There is so much to be gained in Christian life to hear of how God has been at work in the lives of other people, to raise our level of expectation, and to encourage us when the line seems to have gone cold. Paul Harvey has gathered together a rich resource of stories from WEC members around the world from which we can benefit … and perhaps learn how to tell our stories to pass on in turn to others.

ALAN TOWER
National Director, Friends International
(working among international students in the
UK and Ireland: friendsinternational.uk)

The dust and sweat, the blood and tears of the long campaign of Kingdom advance are all through these stories. Like Mary Magdalene, who ran to tell the disciples she had seen the risen Christ, the faithful, ordinary men and women in *Only One Life* have seen Christ alive and at work in our day in the power of His rising – and are eager for us to see Him, too.

TIM KEESEE
Director of Frontline Missions International;
Executive Producer of the *Dispatches from the Front* film series;
Author, *A Company of Heroes*

In a world preoccupied with the spectacular and superheroes, it is easy to lose sight of the wonderful work God is doing daily in different places. He works through ordinary people and often in ordinary ways. *Only One Life* is, in many ways, a call to praise and give thanks to God by recounting his wondrous works among, through, in and for his people. Read these simple stories and behold God's matchless love and power.

CHOPO MWANZA
Pastor, Faith Baptist Church, Kitwe, Zambia

This book is a striking record both of the heroism of many godly women and men, and also, helpfully global mission has meant and can n

T0016776

also it will show you God; I have been blessed by the many stories it contains of God's direct intervention, especially in the section on Prayer, and also some of quite remarkable church growth!

PETE LOWMAN
Former coordinator of the pioneering CU
movements in five post-Soviet republics, and author
of IFES' history *The Day of His Power*

For the most part, the gospel of the Kingdom does not spread through huge stadium events, or even through remarkable spiritual breakthroughs. It spreads like yeast, kneaded through the dough, and producing a long, slow rise. The testimonies herein are examples of this exact principle. God uses ordinary but faithful people to permeate needy places with the good news – through their ministries, through their prayers, sometimes through the miracles He works through them, but always through the impact of lives devoted to loving God and loving people. Eugene Peterson's aptly-named *A Long Obedience in the Same Direction* states, 'Each act of obedience by the Christian is a modest proof, unequivocal for all its imperfection, of the reality of what he attests.' The WEC missionaries in this publication are an example for the rest of us because their obedience to God, lived out transculturally, offers those proofs – that the good news of Jesus is real, is good, and produces real change in our lives and the lives of others.

JASON MANDRYK
Lead Researcher and Author, *Operation World*

MISSIONS STORIES FROM
AROUND THE WORLD

ONLY ONE LIFE

ED. PAUL M. HARVEY

CHRISTIAN
FOCUS

To all of WEC's retired members, past
and present, who have served the Lord in
cross-cultural ministry.

*One generation will commend Your works to another,
they will tell of Your mighty acts.*

Psalm 145:4

FOREWORD

David Northcote

For any Christian setting out to serve the Living God it can seem a daunting prospect, but what is often forgotten is the sheer excitement of a blank canvas on which our Creator will replicate Himself in a multitude of ways. We may be like the child who once remarked, 'I want to see God with skin on.'

Each one who has contributed to this publication has added to my understanding of who God is and how He works. Their testimonies inspired me when I joined WEC International bound for the Far East, and they continue to inspire today.

One thing is clear: their ability to inspire is undiminished by the passage of time; it is their attitude to life when obstacles and difficulties arise, often in the face of failing faculties, that stands out. You rarely hear them talk about themselves or what they have done but whenever we attend a thanksgiving service following a home-call, we are humbled to discover all that they have been involved in.

These are snippets taken from some of these individual lives, told in their own words, that will help you to appreciate how that faith, perseverance, fortitude, humility and humour were formed in them.

INTRODUCTION

Paul M. Harvey

The stories in this collection describe real-life experiences from around the world. They tell about:

- God's protection – in times of war, on journeys, from enemy attacks, in everyday life …
- Prayer – for daily needs, for help in trouble, for rain (or no rain) as the occasion demanded …
- God's providence – through dreams, through circumstances, through His over-riding care …
- People – both God's servants and those they went to serve, their characters and cultures …

Why do we share stories? To entertain, to encourage, to inspire …

These stories hopefully do all this, but they do more. They speak about ordinary people serving an extra-ordinary God who delights to demonstrate His love in and through them.

The Bible talks of how God's people shared their stories of faith from generation to generation: 'One generation will commend Your works to another, they will tell of Your mighty acts' (Ps. 145:4). This same spirit of faith prompts us today to put our simple stories down in writing so that others who follow might be built up and encouraged.

WEC – Worldwide Evangelization for Christ, is a Mission Organization founded by C. T. Studd and Alfred Buxton in 1913 (originally the Heart of Africa Mission). There are nearly 2000 full-time members from over fifty nations working in seventy-plus locations around the globe. WEC UK & Ireland is made up of several hundred active members plus about 160 retired members (mostly as active as ever!).

C. T. Studd knew the importance of inspiring the next generation. He was a prolific writer, constantly exhorting others to serve the Living God. The following extract, taken from a letter which he wrote from the heart of Africa to his grandchildren back in England, reveals his passion to spur others on to make their lives count for Jesus:

> I shall evidently never have the joy of seeing you with these natural eyes nor of speaking to you, but that makes me long to write my heart to you. I may never again have the opportunity. God has taken me to many parts of this world and I have met many people, and I want to give you all the results of what experience I have obtained: and so I plunge in at once. My loving advice to you is summed up in a few lines which I want you to learn by heart:

INTRODUCTION

Only one life, 'twill soon be past;
Only what's done for Jesus will last.[1]

I hope you enjoy these stories, and that they'll inspire you to live the one life you have, for Jesus!

---

1. Quoted from '**Fool & Fanatic? Quotations from the letters of C. T. Studd'**, edited by Jean Walker, ebook 2013 by Smashwords edition, from Chapter 18: A Farewell Letter to his Grandchildren, p. 65.

PROTECTION

The name of the Lord is a strong tower
(Prov. 18:10)

THE ESCAPE

Margaret Davies

The civil war had erupted two weeks earlier in this normally peaceful, even optimistic, yet poor, West African country. We were surprised it had lasted so long already, but now troops from neighbouring countries were pouring in to support the President whose own army had rebelled. Because of this 'help', the war in Guinea-Bissau was to go on for a year, but we weren't to know that at the time.

The United Nations had sent ships to evacuate all foreigners over a week before and most of the missionaries in the capital had left. Six of us had stayed to look after the property, feeling sure the fighting would not last long. But daily we saw the city emptying, as missiles were fired indiscriminately into the residential area around us. Most shops were closed with nothing left to sell. The few still open kept their metal grills closed all day and served the clients through the grill. A few brave women came in to sell their garden produce daily, but there were few customers left in this ghost town that had always been a heaving mass of humanity.

It seemed the military had a regular siesta after lunch as the bombings ceased for a few hours.

After hours of diving under the table every time one heard the whizzing of a rocket, it was a relief to get out for a few hours to see who was left of the neighbours – mostly only old men, who couldn't face the trudge across the fields to goodness-knows-where, and were left to guard the homes of the extended family. Some had come to me for help with the wounded, but I had no experience with shrapnel wounds and felt very inadequate. All I could do with any confidence was give out antibiotics and painkillers.

So, on the advice of the national church pastors, it was decided we should leave in the Land Rover before dawn when the roadblocks would be put in situ. A message was sent to friends on an island. One man had his own canoe, and he would come and collect us off a beach twenty miles from where we were. We had to take as much food as we could. The Land Rover keys were later to be left in a pre-arranged hiding place where a pastor would find them and take the Land Rover away. Simple. We cooked food for the day and left it in a pressure cooker for easy transport. How we thanked God later for that providential guidance!

Though it was still dark with, of course, no electricity, we soon became aware that the road was crammed with a seething mass of humanity – like ants fleeing from danger – all desperate to escape the city. Almost everyone carried a child on her back or on his shoulders. Each woman had a huge plastic basin with as many of their possessions as possible on her head – clothes, pots and pans, bedding and long, rolled-up straw bed-mats, and of course, rice, the essential to life. As dawn broke, we were driving through villages that flanked the road and saw thousands of people lying on the verandahs and in the houses, starting to stir.

It was raining, so people huddled for shelter wherever they could. The eerie silence was such a contrast to the boisterous, good-natured banter we were used to. We stopped briefly at the village where some leprosy sufferers lived to give them some money. There were few dry eyes when we left. Who would help them now?

The sun was rising high as the first rockets came whizzing overhead, exploding at random.

Pandemonium broke out as people dived for cover. In the chaos, parents and children were separated. We heard some families were still searching for their children days later, searching with renewed hope whenever a new batch of people arrived on the beach, for that was where everyone was heading. Some people came loaded on trucks, but most on foot.

Once at the beach, canoes and boats were not frequent – each taking far more than their capacity. Again, parents and children would get separated, and often they wouldn't know where the boat their relatives had embarked on was going. We white folk would never have been able to fight our way on to these fragile looking vessels, but of course, we knew that we were due to be picked up.

Unfortunately though, our friend had left in his boat for another island, so he didn't receive our message until he returned, a week later. That was when our pressure cooker of food proved such a blessing!

The beach was simply a narrow strip, especially when the tide was in, almost covering it completely. It was bordered by mangrove swamps. There was no shade in the heat of the day or shelter from the rain which usually came at night. The two oldest ladies of our group, both over seventy, opted to sleep in the car, while the rest of us slept on the beach – quite pleasant at times, but not very restful for a week. The few nights it rained we ran to the car, as did dozens of other people, all passing their babies and toddlers in through the windows. What a scramble it was afterwards to try and get them back to their own mothers!

Water was desperately short, and our one male took the container and queued for more every morning. Fortunately, the kind pastor from the city who had been entrusted with collecting the mission pick-up, brought tanks of water from our own well every day. All day, every day, trucks brought hundreds more people, but many, once they saw the conditions, returned the way they had come. Some of us organised meetings for the children where they played games, sang and heard Bible stories. Some were deeply traumatised by things they had seen and by the constant noise of explosions and firing that was far from comforting.

Eventually, our canoe arrived, and we piled in. The captain was strict, however, so only thirty could come on board. Many hands helped us with our luggage and I soon discovered that someone had helped themselves to my hold-all with all my worldly goods. It's surprising what you can do without when you have to!

We found the island to be almost sinking under the weight of the people arriving every day.

The population had multiplied many times over already and still they came. Food supplies were dangerously low. A white boat-owner offered to take us to Dakar in Senegal for about £1000 – he was trying to recuperate the money he had lost from the last load who hadn't paid him. But we had to get to Dakar somehow – our leader had had no news of his pregnant wife and three children who were waiting anxiously there for him.

So, after another week, our journey continued. A speed boat took us and many others in relays out to a Portuguese military aircraft carrier which was on its way to an oil rig to refuel. We were warmly welcomed aboard and made as comfortable as possible on deck. It was about 2:00 a.m. when the refuelling started, and the seas were rough. I wondered how we would cross over to another boat which would take us further. Just looking at the waves made me feel dizzy. But a solution was at hand in the form of a helicopter. Thank you, Lord!

Again, many 'Benvindus' (welcome) from the kind sailors, though this boat had already filled up in the city port, so even a place on the floor was difficult to find. It was lashing freezing rain. Our group were good sailors fortunately, but not all the other passengers were. There was a whole orphanage on board – all babies – so when we eventually did get into dock in Cape Verde there was a huge reception with TV cameras. We were all kept waiting while each baby in turn was carried down the steps by a sailor.

There we were all officially registered as 'Refugees' and given a number which was hung around our necks. All refugees were being housed in an unoccupied psychiatric hospital out in the wilds, with not a blade of grass in sight. It doesn't rain in Cape Verde. It looked like a moonscape with hills covered in ancient volcanic rocks. Thankfully, our stay there was only a few days – lack of water was again the main problem.

Soon, the refugee organization arranged a flight for us to Dakar – the Africans who had no definite family or friends to receive them were less fortunate. We'd heard nothing from the British Consulate, whom I assume had left when the first shot had been fired a month before. As it happened, this worked in our favour as we neither had the air fares nor an official Embassy. We therefore flew for free, while the one German was told he'd have to pay back his Embassy when he got home.

What a welcome awaited us – particularly for the father-of-three – as all our colleagues met us at Dakar airport!

Our accommodation was again grossly overcrowded, so I quickly made plans to continue on to The Gambia by bus. That brought the modes of transport for our getaway to eight! Although I and some of the others had, in true British style, considered the whole adventure something of a lark, once I made it to The Gambia the reaction set in. I vomited for several days nonstop, proving myself a mere mortal after all. However, I believe during this time I was closer to the Africans and to God than ever before.

Postscript

It would be a year before the President of Guinea-Bissau was ousted and allowed to leave the country on health grounds. Few other deposed dictators have been so lucky.

I returned 'home' after about six months to the south of the country, where there was no fighting. The return journey by land was less exciting than my departure though not without its moments.

I found our village packed with refugees from the city, mostly staying with distant cousins they hardly knew. My house – a sitting room and three bedrooms – was fully occupied, with one family of seven in one room and an indeterminate number of young people filling everywhere else.

At least they had not been idle. They had managed to grow mountains of peanuts which, now that they had been harvested, had to be dried. So, they were piled up in the sitting room most of the time. Inevitably they had attracted other uninvited guests – rats love peanuts, so they were everywhere. At least it was good to be home.

The next problem was ... besides peanuts, what were we going to eat? And, how to cook it? No oil, no gas, very little charcoal, which I'd never used before. Another new skill to learn. It is at times like this when you discover who your friends are!

Soon, the city people started to drift back home as the danger was almost over. Our little village shrank back to its peaceful self. My Land Rover was returned to me intact. Most cars had been confiscated by the military and were never returned but mine had had a busy time distributing food supplies by famine agencies, as I had left it in the care of a missionary in the south.

God is faithful. You never really know it until you go through the tests.

Margaret Davies served in Guinea-Bissau from 1986–2004 in both midwifery and evangelism roles. The civil war lasted from June 1998 to May 1999, during which about 3,000 foreign nationals were evacuated by ship to Senegal. An unknown number of nationals were killed, and about 350,000 displaced.

STRONG TOWER
Olive Howard

(IVORY COAST – WEST AFRICA 1988)

The name of the Lord is a strong tower,
The righteous run to it and are safe.
(Prov. 18:10)

In our town in the forest region where I worked as a Bible translator among an unreached people group, there lived a man possessed by unclean evil spirits. At certain seasons of the moon, he became very vocal, roaming around the town. People kept their distance ...

His family lived in our neighbourhood at the top of a hill. We'd hear him passing on the road. On our property we had two bungalows, and, at that time, we were four lady missionaries living there. Two of us were long-term and two were new arrivals to Africa, staying with us for a while to learn the culture and become acclimatised to African life. We each had a new arrival living with us.

This man had spent some time receiving help and Biblical counselling at the prayer centre in the north of the country – but he would not obey their rules and was asked to leave. So, he returned home to our town again, unchanged.

Late one afternoon, we heard him on the hill, shouting. Arriving in front of our gates, he stopped and started rattling the gates to open them, yelling: 'I'm going to kill them!' The four of us ran quickly into our houses, locking the doors before he got into our yard. We had two large barrels filled with water installed on a tower, providing water for our houses (there was no running water system in the town at that time). He made for the pipes and broke them – all the water poured down. Then he came over and started banging on the wooden panels of my front door – still shouting. The panels began to give way and I could see him through the cracks!

I started shouting, 'Go away! Go away!' but to no effect. Then I yelled: 'IN THE NAME OF JESUS GO AWAY!' Immediately his hands dropped limply to his sides – not another murmur. He turned to leave through our gate. Then he noticed our car parked, and some new bricks drying alongside.

He picked up three and threw them at the car. One hit the roof, the second broke a window and the third one missed. He left and walked home ...

Neighbours came round to see what had happened, and to assess the damage. By now it was dusk. We saw that we would need a carpenter right away to repair the door – one came quickly, to make the house secure for the night. Then it started raining. We stopped to praise the Lord for answered prayer – we were all safe, unharmed. The Lord truly was our strong tower!

We phoned our Field Leader to report what had happened, and the next day he sent one of the team down to check up on us all. That night God gave us peace in our hearts, and we slept well. The following day we did a prayer walk round our property, praising God and claiming His protection.

The culprit passed our gate often, but never tried to enter again. Proverbs 18 verse 10 was our salvation. Hallelujah!

On 7ᵗʰ July 1958, Olive Howard boarded the 'Niger Palm' at Tilbury Docks, London, bound for the Ivory Coast (Côte d'Ivoire). She served in evangelism, teaching and Bible translation, and returned to the UK in 2001. Thereafter, she headed up regular Parents' Days to support parents of missionaries on the field.

3

CRASH!

Margaret White

I was a missionary teacher in Ibambi, north-east Zaire (now the Democratic Republic of the Congo). Our nearest town for supplies was Isiro, fifty miles away over a horrendously bad road. Before each trip, the African Christians would pray with us for a safe journey.

On 15th September 1985, my friend Beryl and I had just completed our monthly shop with reasonable success and were heading to lunch with friends on the outskirts of town before tackling the long road home. An old narrow-gauge railway track runs through the town but there was no longer a regular train service, just an occasional engine. It crosses the road quite a lot, but nobody pays any attention to it. There are no level crossings. As we passed the Post Office, we noticed a stationary diesel engine, with number 91 at the front and 92 at the back. My letter from home said my four-year-old nephew had started trainspotting with my Dad, and we laughingly wondered which number they would note in this case.

I was driving towards the long grass near the stadium, one of the places where the road crosses the track, when beside me Beryl screamed. I braked and stalled. The train was suddenly right there! Bang! We went flying through the air, with me frantically braking and steering (useless, of course) so that it wouldn't hit us a second time. We both thought, 'This is it. Here we come, Lord.'

Then, 'You okay?'

'Yes. You?'

'Yes. Just glass in my hair. Let's get out of here.'

A crowd quickly came running and yelling at the train driver. We realised he was in danger of being attacked by the mob, so we screamed in every language we knew to leave him alone. It wasn't his fault. The local military commander, General Yossa, arrived, dispersed the crowd, and took us to our friends.

He got our two American nurse friends to come and check that we were okay. We ended up staying the night with them. I can still see their dinner table that evening, set for a feast, with pink table cover, candles and glasses, flowers and a cake with gleaming chocolate frosting like in a magazine.

'Are you celebrating something?' we asked.

'Sure! We're celebrating that you girls are able to be with us this evening. Thank You, Father, for answered prayer, and keeping these girls safe.'

The next day, when we saw the Land Rover, crumpled and with a badly buckled chassis, we couldn't believe we had come out of that mess alive. Thank You, Lord.

Radio Message: 'Nobody was hurt, but the Ibambi Land Rover was hit by a train in Isiro.'

Margaret White served in Zaïre (now the Democratic Republic of Congo) from 1970–1996, first in the secondary school to help young Christians enter the professions, and then travelling to the village churches for discipleship and mission awareness seminars.

VOICES FROM SENEGAL

Collated by Sheila Kilkenny

The following are tributes read at Patrick Underwood's thanksgiving service ...

Pastor Joseph Lambal:

I love Pat Underwood. I had an unhappy home life and my parents divorced. As a young boy, I was looking for a love that no-one could give me. One evening, I went to the Underwoods' place and after the games Pat took us into the little chapel and spoke to us of the love of Jesus Christ. And I received it. Pat was for me a loving father, with many qualities. I used to confide in him about all my problems, and he always referred me to the Lord Jesus Christ. Patrick was a man of God, loving Him with all of his being.

Pastor Ouffi Boly:

Thank you for all of you who keep in touch and pray for us, you the pioneers who proclaimed the Gospel to the Jola people in the Casamance. God bless all those of you who are still alive: I can assure you, and all those who are present to honour Pat Underwood, that we will continue to work so that this Light continues to shine in the darkness of the Jola people until Jesus returns.

I wept a lot when Lorna died. I had so many memories in my head and so much emotion in my heart with a profound feeling of gratitude towards the Underwood family who looked on me as a member of their family. However, for Pat I haven't wept. Instead, I experience feelings of Glory. Sheila told me of the advanced state of his illness when I was in Mali for evangelism amongst people who are being massacred because they belong to Jesus. When I received the news, I prayed that the Lord would receive to Himself His devoted servant Pat Underwood. And today I thank Him for doing it. I live in the assurance that they gave us and know that one day we shall be together again because, for us, death is not a mystery.

The leaders of the church at Diembering have always considered Pat as head pastor. When I began my ministry at Ziguinchor, Pat came from time to time to audit the mission accounts and, when he visited believers at Diembering, I accompanied him. Every time when the doors opened and the believers realised it was Pat, huge smiles lit up their faces. One said to me, 'This man and his wife were so good to us and I don't know how to explain it all.' The Underwood family didn't only teach the Gospel to the believers at Diembering but helped them to get a fishing project up and running to improve their living conditions. It was during one of these visits that I asked Pat what work he came out to do for WEC both in The Gambia and in Senegal. He told me that he came to audit the books. So I said, you must be an expert accountant and you never told us! His reply was something I've never forgotten: 'It's like Moses: God made me throw away the rod of my profession. And then I took it up again in His service.' Today, he is with the Lord and will receive the crown of Glory from the hands of Christ.

The other memory linked to my personal life is when I was dragged out into the Atlantic Ocean at Diembering. My big brother William ran straight to Pat to look for help because he was frightened that if he ran home, he'd get into trouble for taking me to the sea. But he trusted Pat and Lorna! And it's thanks to the quick reaction of Pat that God saved me from drowning. In fact, how can a boy about eight years of age who can hardly swim survive at least three hours in the sea? I was so far out that all the tallest person on the beach could see was my head, bobbing like a life belt! Pat was among those who swam to help me, with a rope. But I was so far out that some of them had to give up or wait for another person in the relay to reach them. It was a man from the village, young at the time, who finally reached me and got me out.

The fact that I survived was an answer to prayer and the hand of God. Graham and Mary Smith were close friends of the Underwoods, and Mary said when telling her Sunday School class about it, that God had sent His angel. Yes, it was a miracle of God that the Jola people witnessed because our traditional gods do not save. Instead, they require blood sacrifices.

In closing, I pray that all present today will experience the deep, inexplicable feeling of peace and calm when faced with death, which is no mystery when one has the faith that Pat and Lorna had. In particular, I pray that their children and grandchildren will accept Jesus Christ whom their parents went to serve in the village that was called, at the time, the end of the earth.

Albert and Irma Diatta:

Dear brothers and sisters in Christ, we were sad to hear of the passing of Pastor Patrick Underwood. On behalf of the evangelical church of Diembering and the entire Kwatay Christian community, I present our sincere condolences to WEC in general and in particular to his children, Paul, David and Jenny. May God comfort you.

Pastor Patrick was not only a source of blessing to us but also to the entire Diembering church. We will never forget all the good things that he accomplished from the start of his ministry. God has given us a harvest where they planted seed, all the missionaries who served at Diembering: the Kennedys, the Underwoods, Mademoiselles Mena and Pamela laboured here – and we have entered into their labours. As Jesus said: 'He who sows and he who reaps rejoice together' (John 4:36).

It's wonderful to know that a crown of life is Pat's for eternity!

Patrick and Lorna Underwood served in Senegal from 1965–1986, then as Regional Coordinators for the Southwest UK region until 2004. Patrick went to Glory in 2020.

Sheila Kilkenny served in Senegal from 1967 till the late 80s.

5

FLYING COFFINS AND DESERT ROADS

Meg Northcote

(*Pseudonyms are used for security reasons)

All attempts to have someone travel with me on my second trip to Canland* back in 1996 came to nothing, so I found myself planning this visit to the team alone. I was encouraged by a couple who had not long returned from working with the team there to fly with Canland Airlines* as they were the least expensive. After five hours we touched down in Cyprus to be told we had a burst tyre and would be taken to a hotel. It was twenty-four hours before we took off for Canland. When the plane didn't arrive in Canland on time and my host, Hans, who had gone to the airport to meet me, was told they had no news when it would arrive or why it was delayed; he became concerned and phoned the team in the north. Knowing the airline had a poor reputation for reliability, their anxiety increased to the point of phoning Bulstrode, our headquarters in the UK, to make sure I had left!

After a long wait at the airport the next day, the relief on Hans' face was visible when we eventually met. It was then that I learned the team referred to planes used by this airline as 'flying coffins.' I had never received a warmer welcome in my many travels!

Two midwives on the team in the north had set up a clinic in a village two hours from Sandfort* to help the local women and children who would otherwise have to make the long trip to the hospital late in pregnancy to give birth. The midwives had been well received but, just a few days before I arrived, a bomb was thrown at their home. Neither was hurt as they were in another part of the house attending a local woman who had called for medication that evening. Local people were horrified at the incident and were determined to find the culprit.

When I arrived at the hospital in Sandfort where the team worked, these two ladies had arrived from the village for supplies of medications as well as food. It was two years since my last visit, but this hardly seemed the time for these ladies to be taking me back to see how the project was going. However, after two days we packed the vehicle and the three of us set off over the mountains back to the village. When we arrived, we discovered that soldiers had been posted around the house from sundown and remained there till morning. When we opened up the clinic next morning the tension of the bomb incident filled the conversations. Who could have done such an evil thing? Some were amazed that the two midwives had returned and even brought a visitor with them! The following day, as we were having breakfast, there was a gunshot outside our gate! We could hear raised voices and felt it was better to stay inside.

I began to sing 'The Name of the Lord is a strong tower; the righteous run to it and they are safe' and spontaneously the two midwives joined in. We started to praise Him together and felt so safe despite not being able to call the hospital – mobile phones were not around then, and the radio was out of action, but it didn't matter; we felt very safe. We were *in* the 'Strong Tower.' Soon, there was a knock at the door and the son of the local Imam was there to explain what was happening at the gate.

A disgruntled doctor from a neighbouring country had arrived in the area a few weeks previously and was not happy to find these two midwives had set up a clinic to serve the poor with negligible charges for their services. This had resulted in his clinic not going well owing to the higher charges he demanded. He was so angry he thought he would scare them out of the area! Therefore, the son of the Imam, certain of the doctor's complicity with the bombing, took it into his head to shoot at the tyres of the doctor's car as a warning to him to stay away from these midwives. Since he wanted to make sure we were safe he insisted on travelling with us on our return trip to Sandfort* the next day with his loaded gun between me and him! One of the midwives was able to witness to him during that trip back.

My return journey to the capital city involved a ten-hour trip by road through the notorious desert mountains, so it was a comfort to have one of the midwives travel with me in the taxi to the airport.

I noticed she circled the waiting taxis, paying particular attention to the state of their tyres before negotiating with the driver. There was little to choose between them as they all would have failed an MOT test in UK, but having decided on the best of them we took the last two places and hopped in. The driver had to close the door from the outside as many components were absent. About two hours into the trip, it became obvious that the brakes were incapable of an emergency stop as we trundled down a hill with increasing pace. With our nerves shattered, the road levelled out and we stopped at a village where a mechanic was sought.

Having resumed our journey some hours later, we were approaching sundown, miles from a living soul, when we heard much spluttering coming from under the bonnet and suddenly the engine cut out. The other six passengers flagged down other cars passing and bagged all the spare room they had, so now we were on our own with the driver. With the onset of night, we were glad of our light jackets to protect us from the plummeting temperatures. Many kidnappings occur on this stretch of desert, but the driver was trusting for another taxi to help him get the vehicle going again. As chilling thoughts came into our heads so did the chorus we had sung together earlier and peace and certainty that the Lord would deliver us took control.

Help can come in many forms. For us, a taxi did eventually stop, and the guy looked under our bonnet and asked us to pass him a large rock from the side of the road. Amazingly a blow to the engine was all that was required for it to splutter into life once again. Our next problem was the lack of headlights that became apparent as we headed off into the night on bendy mountainous roads. At the sight of the city lights of the capital we both shouted 'Hallelujah' in unison! Our anxious team hosts in the north had called to see if we had arrived, so imagine their relief when we finally rolled into town and were able to ring and let them know we had safely arrived.

As prayer co-ordinator for the team, sharing with the UK Prayer Groups, this trip brought to life the reality of all that the team faced in working in such a dangerous place, and with it the amazing opportunities they were given to share the Good News of Jesus.

Among other roles over the years, Meg Northcote (née Booth) was International Prayer Co-ordinator for the Middle East and North Africa from 1995–2010.

LOBI FUNERAL

Jo Parnell

'Well, we were never expecting this!' I thought as Margaret and I were sitting in a very hot, flat-roofed mud church in the hill country of southeast Burkina Faso. Right near us, in the centre of this small 'God's Greeting House,' seated on a chair, dressed in his best clothes, was the body of a man, a recent believer in Jesus, who had died unexpectedly the night before. Several women believers sat with us as we were practically deafened by the noise outside.

Their men folk were continuing to dig the grave that they had started four hours before. These were all relatively new believers who were standing firm in the face of hostility from their family and neighbours. The latter were angry that this small group of Christians had dared to leave the traditions of their tribe, had destroyed their idols and were following some unknown God called Jesus.

So there they were outside, encircling the church, noisily demanding to have the body. They needed to question it in order to find out the reason for his death. They had chickens with them that they needed to sacrifice to the Earth in order to have permission to bury the body, and cowrie shells for him to take into the next world. The musicians were there with their drums and xylophones. The men were shouting and brandishing their bows and arrows whilst the women were wailing and dancing for the dead. But to no avail, as these Christians wouldn't allow it and they had no fear of repercussions from the demons. To add to it these two white women had come to reinforce them. They must have known!

We had set off that morning on the twenty-five kilometre journey on our Mobylettes (a make of moped) in order to join the church for their service and to bring something from God's Word. Language study was well behind me, and I was now able to give a simple message. I had been practising it, but it certainly wasn't right for this occasion! Margaret, a short-term worker, had very little of the language. 'Where in Thessalonians does it talk about the resurrection from the dead?' was also going through my mind. I had a Lobi New Testament with me and started to think of what I would say.

After three hours (weren't we glad we had plenty of water with us to drink!) the men reported the grave was ready (a simple six-by-four), very different by far from the usual tribal way of doing things. The heathen, now quiet, watched fearfully from the distance, as the body was laid into the grave and then covered with earth, and as we sang the only song we had for such a time as this: 'If we die, we will rise again!' A layer of mud, which would soon set hard in the sun, was applied and then covered by a layer of rocks which would hopefully protect the grave from animal or human interference. I read 1 Thessalonians 4:13-18, comforting the bereaved family and this brave band of believers with 'these words' (v. 18).

I thought that I knew the heathen practices regarding funerals, but as we made to leave, the grave diggers came and asked if they could wash. Apparently, the heathen only wash after a week and further sacrifices. No need for that! Then we needed to set off as it was getting late and sunset was at 6:00 p.m. As we followed our guide on his bike up and down the winding hilly paths to the main road, I thought again, 'We were certainly not expecting that, but – thank you, Lord! – we were privileged to be there with our faithful brothers and sisters.'

'We believe that Jesus died and rose again and so we believe that God will bring with Jesus those who have fallen asleep in him.' (I Thess. 4:14)

Jo Parnell worked in Burkina Faso, West Africa, from 1970–1992 in a teaching and training capacity in literacy, children's work and supporting pastors and their wives.

7

YOUR HOUSE FELL DOWN

Liz Cleak

It seemed like a normal day in Chad. I'd been up in the capital city staying with friends for just over a week, a welcome break as I was living alone in the Barma village where my colleague Pauline and I had a base. This was ninety-five miles away along a poorly maintained road, and fifteen miles from any shops, so I was laying in supplies to last for a while. Nothing other than local produce was available in the weekly village market. During Pauline's absence on leave, village life was very busy with many demands on my time.

We had come to this village to learn the unwritten Barma language with a view to translating key passages from the Bible. We felt very much at home and welcome in this remote village community where local people were eager to teach us their language and culture, but we were constantly aware of other needs where they hoped for our help. Like basic healthcare, schooling, commerce ...

With help and advice from the nearest hospital, I stocked some basic medicines for malaria, fever, diarrhoea, etc. A group of the young men had asked us to teach them French, so that they could better cope with paperwork when trading across the nearby border. Clinic, classroom, social contact, all took place on the shady verandah at the front of our house.

A Dutch colleague had designed and helped to oversee the construction of this mud brick thatched house, just to one side of the main village and on a cliff beside the Chari River. We had spectacular views across the river valley. However, it was a windy site and we had already experienced some problems with the roof as the wind got under the eaves, partly lifting it off one stormy night! We were also permanently watching out for termites which enjoyed doing a sprint up the walls overnight, aiming for wooden furniture or roof beams to munch on. Let's say it was a high maintenance house! In our absences we employed two older men, well respected in the community, to sleep at the property, keep watch over it and feed our animals.

So having packed our small Suzuki jeep to the gills, I collected the village friend who had come with me to the capital, and set off on the long, hot journey home. Usually this would take about five hours or so. Before leaving the capital, I filled up at a service station; strong and mostly reliable as the brilliant little Suzy was, she was particularly fussy about clean fuel. All went well until about two hours into the trip I realised this fuel must have been dirty ... the jeep was coughing and spluttering and living up to its nickname of 'sauterelle' (grasshopper) and even regularly grinding to a halt.

Each time this happened, one could try rinsing the fuel filter (we always carried a jerrycan of extra petrol and cloths to filter it) or even changing it, although often a short stop would allow the fuel in the tank to settle with the dirty residue at the bottom so that one could travel another stretch before becoming a sauterelle again.

It was dusk when we finally arrived at the small village near the main road where we had a small shelter for the car. Huge sighs of relief! I should explain that the final stage of our journey home was always crossing by dugout canoe across the Chari river, which varied in size according to the season. We had our own canoe and even our own faithful boatman, Moussa, who was there to meet us.

He had seen the lights of the Suzy on the main road. I was so glad to see him, late as the hour was, as I was exhausted after that journey.

Moussa's first words were, 'Your house fell down!' I'm sure you can imagine my feelings at that moment! I think it was one of my lowest points in village life. But the only thing to be done in the gathering dusk was to load up the canoe and get across the river before nightfall.

Once there, it turned out to be a bit less disastrous than it had first sounded. It seemed that during a freak storm the night before, the guards heard ominous cracking sounds from my end of the house and realised that the end wall (the most exposed to wind and weather) was splitting away from the rest of the building. Bless them, they ran to save my bits of furniture and possessions. They hastily stuffed them all across the yard into the small room we used as storage. The last item to go in was my plastic wardrobe. Not made to be carried full of clothes, it collapsed in the doorway and blocked entry to the room, so that evening on arrival I just collapsed fully clad on the bed in Pauline's room and slept there, trusting that life would look better in the light of day. Which it did.

Thankfully, later that year we were able to replace the collapsed part of the house with several small round houses in the local style; much easier to maintain.

Postscript

We had the privilege of communication with colleagues in the capital via a two-way radio system set up by MAF (Mission Aviation Fellowship). So, the following day, I recounted the adventure to my friends over the radio. By the time this story got to the UK someone phoned Pauline, most concerned, as they had heard that our car had broken down, and that on arrival home I'd discovered the river had risen and flooded our house, causing it to collapse. The thought of the river rising up the thirty-foot cliff always amused us!

Liz Cleak served in Chad from 1976–2000, living among the unreached Barma people for about fifteen years; for part of that time, she was also co-leader of the Chad branch of WEC.

8

JUST IN THE NICK OF TIME

Sue Frampton

When we had been in Ghana for a few months, living in the north, we came down to the guest house in Accra. I was in the guest house along with my two younger children, and David was out in the Land Rover taking care of some business. The guest house managers were also out. Suddenly Daniel, then four years old, went over the handlebars of his bike and split his chin from side to side. It was a big, gaping hole. The time was coming up to 5:00 p.m., and I knew that the one doctor at the hospital which we had used before, and which was recommended, would be leaving soon.

I prayed that someone would come to take us to the hospital before the doctor left. I expected either David or the guest house managers to return. But God had another plan. At that exact moment, Ross Campbell, a fellow WEC missionary, was driving round the roundabout near the guest house on his way home via a different road. As he drove round, it came into his head, out of the blue, to call on the guest house to see how we were. When he saw Daniel, he scooped us all into his car and drove straight to this same hospital. Since Ross knew his way around, he drove to the back of the hospital and as we parked, we saw the doctor getting into his car in order to go home for the day. We were able to call him, and he came back into the hospital and was able to stitch Daniel up under a general anaesthetic.

If David had brought us, we would have gone to the front of the hospital and missed the doctor.

If we had been two minutes later, we would have missed him, but God's timing is perfect.

Praise the Lord!

Sue and her husband David were in Ghana from 1987–1997. They were in the north, church planting among the Konkomba people. Later on they served in the Middle East. Back in the UK, both Sue and David took 'active retirement' status in WEC, with the emphasis on 'active'!

FIRST YEAR IN GUINEA-BISSAU

Amy Cuthbert

Norman and I, with Jayne who was nine-months old, arrived in Guinea-Bissau on 25th November 1975. After ten days in the capital, Bissau, we went to live on Bubaque island alongside our colleagues Wesley and Frances Lindsay. Bubaque is a five to six-hour boat journey from Bissau.

February 1976 Conference in Orango

Orango island is about three hours from Bubaque by pirogue (a type of canoe). We travelled in the middle of the day. Before we left, Jayne had vomited but we went on anyway. I had never travelled by canoe before so didn't know the importance of getting a good seat and not moving from it! The motor stopped at one stage, so we sat in the open sea (in the midday sun) until that was fixed. Eventually, we arrived. There was a mission house on Orango – it was now a bit run-down and was occupied by the local evangelist, a widower.

There was a small church beside the house, but the villagers had erected a larger shelter for the Conference meetings as Christians from all the other islands would come – about 300-400 of them. It was a time of great rejoicing, fellowship and teaching from the Word of God.

We missionaries and pastor/evangelists all stayed in the mission house. The water was drawn from quite far away so was at a premium. Some of the missionaries even washed in the dish rinse water after it had been used. Everyone 'knew the ropes' except me. I held the children's meetings on the verandah. I hadn't sufficient Creole, nor even Portuguese, to do any Bible story justice but I could tell that Joia, an evangelist's wife and my translator, was making a good job of filling in the gaps!

Jayne had her first birthday in Orango. She was still not too well. She got worse with vomiting and diarrhoea. There was a local nurse on the island but he did not have treatment. We were all praying, especially during one night when she was constantly sick.

The next morning a Russian helicopter landed – the reason it came, we discovered, was to exchange the currency after Independence (helicopters never came to Orango). My colleague Areta asked them if we could have a lift to Bissau and they agreed – just Areta, Jayne and me, they wouldn't take Norman. Within hours we were in Bissau and then at the hospital. The doctor gave some medicine and advised us not to return to the hospital with the baby as there was a lot of sickness about. After a few days, Jayne began to improve.

Praise God for His intervention at exactly the right time! After the conference, Norman came to Bissau and by mid-March we were all able to travel back to Bubaque island.

Early May 1976 Meat from the market

We were due to go back to Orango island with Wesley Lindsay to dig a well closer to the village.

However, one day, meat became available in the market in Bubaque – a rare occurrence. Frances bought some and gave us a piece. Frances put hers in her small freezer but, as we had no fridge or freezer yet, I cooked our piece. It didn't smell or look good to me, but I had heard many missionary tales of meat, covered with flies and sitting in the sun, being eaten … so I cooked it. But I couldn't eat it. Norman did.

He got sick! When Frances opened her freezer the next day her meat was green! It turned out Norman had hepatitis. He was very sick and had to go to the local hospital daily for injections into the stomach for a week. He could barely walk from the house to the pick-up truck. For several weeks he was unable to do anything, he was so exhausted.

Augusto, the Pastor, walked the length of the island – twelve miles – in the mid-day sun in search of green papaya. It was to be boiled and the water drunk as remedy. It was foul tasting, but Norman had a daily dose! It was suggested he eat as many vegetables as possible. This was not garden season, but one man had a garden near the big well. I went to the garden to get some vegetables but there was nothing there that I recognised. No carrots, cabbage, turnip or anything resembling anything I knew!

By mid-June, Norman was still not fit enough to go with Wesley to finish off the work in Orango. By the end of June, he was getting back to work but was still very weak. Eventually, he picked up and was able to go to Bissau for a check-up.

August 1976 Delivery day

Two of my sisters were each expecting their second child in August 1976. So was I. Elizabeth had her son prematurely at the end of June. One Sunday morning in August when all had gone to church, I was having my quiet time. Someone arrived at the door with mail which had come on the boat the day before. This brought news that Edith, my other sister, had had her baby too. So, here was I feeling very alone out in Bubaque, and vulnerable as the 'Christian' doctor who was to have attended the birth had been expelled from Guinea-Bissau. I was in tears but a verse from the Psalm I was reading came into focus ... Psalm 50:15: 'Call on me in the day of trouble. I will deliver you and you will honour me.' Suddenly, I knew that God had it all under control. I just knew that the baby would not be born in the hospital in Bissau, which was not noted for hygiene or competence. I had no idea how it would come about, but God would deliver the baby!

We had to come into Bissau to wait for the birth – a five to six-hour boat journey. On 10th September, I went into labour. Thelma Mills had been detailed to accompany me to hospital to help with translation, so a message was sent across town for her to come to the Mission headquarters. The baby came quickly, so Thelma arrived just in time for her appearance! Two other colleagues were also there when Judith was born in the apartment on the Mission HQ. However, the placenta did not come away, so it was decided I needed to be taken to hospital to have it removed.

We were supposed to meet up with a German lady doctor on arrival, but she did not appear. Instead, two Cuban doctors did (at that time, lots of Cuban trainee doctors came to Guinea Bissau to gain experience). I was taken into a ward. There were other pregnant women there – some, two to a bed with no sheets. I noticed all this. A nurse tried to give me an injection in the back of my hand but could not find a vein. I don't know if she succeeded! Thelma was 'translating' but was so excited that anything I said in English she repeated in English, and what the nurse said in Portuguese she repeated in Portuguese, so neither of us was any the wiser. I could see the funny side of this even though I thought I was dying, and Psalm 23 kept going over and over in my head.

Then the Cuban doctors took charge. The placenta was removed manually. Norman and Thelma were sent home as I should now sleep for a while. I came to consciousness in a large ward when Sue Goodman came to visit me. Sue went home again for replacement clothes and sheets. She assisted me to the bathroom across the hall, but we were soon ankle-deep in water! Very often the hospital did not have water but this time I think the taps would not turn off. Sue also brought a flask of tea and some apple creams she had made. The stewed apples were from dried apples and the cream was not fresh cream, but they tasted great! When Sue reported back to Norman it was decided to discharge me to recuperate back at HQ.

In the meantime, Areta McBride and Laura Tomkins had looked after Jayne, now one-and-a-half, and baby Judith. All was well. Praise God!

Amy and Norman Cuthbert served in Guinea-Bissau 1975–1991 (twelve years on the Bijagós Islands and four years as Field Leaders). On returning home they were WEC Co-ordinators for Ireland 1992–1999; UK Deputies & HQ Managers 1999–2007; Directors for all Ireland 2007–2016 ('officially' retiring in 2011!).

A FLUID SITUATION

Mavis Rodger

I sent an angel before you to guard you on your way, and to bring you to the place I have prepared. (Exod. 23:20)

John and I were in the Middle East for several months. We were giving a helping hand at the Maternity Clinic, though note – not in the delivery room!

One day, John and a colleague, Allan, happened to be standing in the driveway. On her return from the capital city, one of the nurses drove right up to them – and stopped.

Nothing remarkable about that. But when the men lifted up the bonnet, there was not a trace of brake fluid to be found whatsoever! No way should that car have stopped.

Surely an angel nearby and two grateful, unflattened men!

John and Mavis Rodger were Long Term workers making Short Term practical mission trips to various countries on different continents from 1979 to 2002.

11

DOULOS DAYS

Rose Harvey

In my early twenties, well before I joined WEC International, my first missionary experience was with Operation Mobilisation. I spent two years on the *M/V Doulos*, circumnavigating Latin America. Working in the Book Exhibition and then as Ship's Nurse for a year, life was extremely busy, but there were opportunities to go ashore ...

In May 1980, I remember sailing into the magnificent city of Willemstad, capital of Curaçao.

This island is green and rocky with a long spectacular coastline and is situated only sixty-five kilometres away from the Venezuelan mainland. It is a former Dutch colony in the Caribbean with all its distinct Dutch features, architecture, language and culture. *Doulos* was able to dry-dock here for nine days. It was here that I joined a *Doulos* land team and we took a night ferry to Coro, Venezuela. It was a rough sea crossing with high winds and rain. We were relieved to arrive safely in Maracaibo after a speedy three-hour taxi ride (it was exactly a year earlier that I had sat my State Registered Nursing finals in a completely different space and time!). It was so hot and clammy, and it was good to enjoy a siesta in an air-conditioned room that afternoon.

The next day another three-hour taxi ride brought us to Trujillo, in the Andes of Venezuela. Jean and I stayed with a lovely missionary lady in her home. I had my own bedroom without air conditioning, so it was a very hot night. In the darkness, it was very noisy with night visitors/creatures moving/crawling around. It had been bad enough getting used to the thousands of cockroaches which cohabited the *Doulos* and my fears of one day swallowing one and choking to death in the middle of the night! I prayed for grace, and consciously decided to turn over, lie still, and go to sleep. Mercifully, I woke up the next morning unharmed and the noises had ceased.

We took a trip up into the hills to Sabana Larga to help with the Children's Bible Story classes. It was great singing simple choruses with them in Spanish. Their sweet little faces stay with me to this day. Although the mountain scenery was so beautiful, the village was so poor and what a shock I had to witness pigs, chickens, stray dogs and cats running through the people's houses so freely.

Our efforts to return to the *Doulos*, which was now anchored at sea near Maracaibo, along with oil tankers, were perilous. It was evening time, and the sea was very choppy and unpredictable.

A launch was to take us alongside our ship so that we could get aboard. It was so dangerous as the launch and the *Doulos*, being of different sizes, were moving without any synchronisation, making the gangway almost inaccessible. A rope/cable snapped. A heavy pulley fell on the head of one of the launch men who then collapsed across the platform at the back of the launch, almost falling into the turbulent waters. I had been right there standing behind him, so I was able to administer immediate first aid. He was unconscious, so I wiped his nose and reached into his mouth to maintain a clear airway and pulled out a lot of broken teeth and blood. He had a severe wound and depressed skull fracture, and I tried desperately to stem the bleeding with a T-shirt off one of the men's backs. Meanwhile, the launch quickly disconnected from the ship, turned and sped back to port. The ambulance was on the quayside as we arrived and he was quickly placed on a stretcher, loaded into the ambulance and off they went at speed to the nearest hospital. I then started shaking as I looked down at my hands, face and clothes covered in blood. Had I done enough to help him? The accident had been fatal and tragically he left behind a wife and young family. My friend, Rose Hall, had been standing right next to him, waiting to mount the gangway. It could have so easily been her, or even me.

I went over all the exotic things I had seen in my mind. The variety of fruit in Brazil was incredible, and I stupidly tried to eat a juicy mango like an apple, with the skin. My digestion worked overtime after that! Then I bought some cashew fruit from the local market with the nut attached. The fruit is very good but ignorantly I tried to open the nutshell with my teeth and quickly developed burns on my lower lip and fingers from the protective oil which surrounds the nut.

In Belem, we visited a local park/zoo with typical dense Amazonian vegetation. Two black panthers snarled at us while they paced up and down their cage. There were crocodiles, turtles, tortoises, jungle pigs and boars. The monkeys were friendly as they blinked at us with large saucer-like, soulful eyes and heavy white eyeshadow. There was an assortment of snakes, including two pythons. The tropical bird life was simply fabulous in all shapes, sizes and colours. The 'paintwork' really was something to behold. The parrots were a favourite. Two of the same species were quite eye-catching, as one had big dark brown eyes surrounded by bright blue eyeshadow, and its companion had big bright blue eyes surrounded by bright orange eyeshadow. Even the vultures on display had brightly coloured heads.

Poverty was apparent in many places. Children with disfigured feet because their shoes were too small, crates of Coca-Cola to drink because the water was not drinkable, ports spoiled by human rubbish, even in Punta Arenas where the surrounding scenery was white and pristine with snow. There was certainly a thirst for education and part of our service was to provide educational books at low budget prices. I received a typical letter from a little girl which read: 'Dear Rose, I am very glad to see you come to my school. This is the first time I am writing you. I am asking you for a watch, and a doll. Good day to you. Please don't let it be late. Your friend, Desreen.'

Another time, a group of us from *Doulos* decided to climb one of the hills near to the ship in Chile. It was a steep climb even for us, but we soon discovered it was even harder coming down! As we started to make our descent, we heard some men shouting from below us. To our shock and alarm, the Chilean Army had arrived and an armoured truck with a mounted machine gun was pointing straight at us as we looked down the barrel! There was nothing for it than to descend at all haste. It was very steep and shaley without any footing, so we all had to slide down on our bottoms as fast as possible, making no end of clouds of black/grey dust. Thankfully, there was a fluent Spanish speaker in our group who could explain who and what we were. They let us go amicably.

Doulos had her annual dry-dock in Montevideo, Uruguay, so I joined a land team of nine personnel and we travelled in a comfortable overnight bus (eight-hour trip) to a small town called Rio Branco, across country close to the Brazilian border. It was winter and a few of us, including myself, had picked up a nasty eye infection, conjunctivitis. I had already had it a week and despite my best nursing efforts it was not getting any better.

The little struggling church in Rio Branco had asked for a ship team to help them in their outreach. There was not much infrastructure in Rio Branco. The main road was a dirt track and 'the gauchos' rode horseback, tying the reins to a wooden hand pole just like in the TV cowboy westerns. Tumbleweed and clouds of irritating dust blew down the streets. Horses and wooden carts were a regular feature, but there were old models of cars/trucks and bicycles too. With many of the women wearing ankle-length skirts and shawls, it felt bizarre to be in such a place in 1981.

Boonsian, Kay Ching and I stayed with Ruben (the pastor) and his wife, Rita, and their sweet little three-year-old son, Pablito. We three girls had a camp bed each in a large empty cold room. The others stayed in the cold and draughty church building. Each morning Rita would wash clothes by hand in icy cold water in a built-in concrete wash bowl with draining board in the back yard. All she had was a bar of soap and a scrubbing brush. The weather was cruelly cold with a harsh, dusty wind. It was a miserable existence.

We had a busy programme that week: door to door visitation with literature; practical helps; local radio and newspaper presentations; church meetings. During our planning meeting early Wednesday morning, Norman, the Team Leader, prayed for my eyes. 'If they are not better by lunch time today, we will find an optician,' he announced. I felt blessed that the whole team were now onboard with my condition, and I didn't have to carry it alone. Amazingly, quite by accident, we met 'the answer to our prayers' as we arrived at the church midday. She was a lovely Christian lady who insisted upon taking me straight to the hospital where she worked. Kay Ching and Orlin, from Venezuela, came with me for translation. We didn't have to wait and were quickly ushered in to see the doctor in his private offices. He was very pleasant, knew exactly what to prescribe, and all free of charge. I had a fungal eye infection for which he gave me eye drops, a broad-spectrum antibiotic and a special body soap for killing parasitic microbes. We were able to talk to the man about our work and he appeared to be most interested. He graciously accepted our free literature as we left. The treatment certainly worked, and I believe it was all an answer to prayer.

In stark contrast to my situation, I visited a young family who were in Ruben's church. The wife was uneducated and illiterate, and the house was poor and dirty. The eldest daughter had neglected, disfigured feet and all the children really needed a good soak in warm soapy water because they were so grimy. We take clean hot water and baths for granted but there in Rio Branco such resources seemed sadly lacking.

These are just a few of the many memories gathered during my *Doulos* experience, which was destined to launch me into a lifetime of missionary service.

Rose Harvey (then Rosemary Scott) served with Operation Mobilisation from 1980–83. After marrying Paul in 1986, she joined WEC International in 1992.

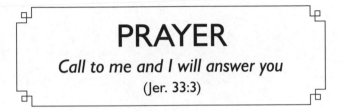

PRAYER

Call to me and I will answer you
(Jer. 33:3)

ON THE ROAD IN GUINEA-BISSAU

Margaret Davies

Driving in the wet season in Guinea-Bissau was always an adventure. In a heavy shower, a 'road' with deep ditches running in all directions could become a riverbed in minutes, so you couldn't see where the holes were. Sometimes, an obliging young man would walk in front of the Land Rover showing us how to avoid tipping over into a ditch. As the season progressed the roads turned to mud, and only four-wheel-drive vehicles would attempt to use them. It was often scary.

One day we were returning from the capital, so we were loaded up with calor-gas bottles, jerry cans of diesel, as well as various provisions of food, flour, sugar and rice (if there was none left at the village where I lived) – not to mention four passengers. About ten miles from home, we got stuck in the mud. Every able-bodied person in the nearby villages came out to help, cutting branches to put under the wheels and pushing. Everyone was covered in mud from head to foot, but to no avail.

When all else fails, pray! Why didn't I think of that before?

Suddenly, coming towards us from the direction of our village was a tractor. Seeing a tractor on this road was like seeing a UFO in South Wales! I've never seen one before or since on that stretch of road, though there was a rumour that there was a project fifty miles due south, where a tractor was in use. Why was it here today? It seemed he was looking for a particular mechanic who could make a part he needed – and that same mechanic just happened to be in the car with me! So, to get it fixed, the driver would have to turn around and pull us out of the mud.

By now, the wheels had almost disappeared. The tow rope I had with me snapped like cotton thread, but the tractor had something stronger and we were soon on our way home. Apart from the fact that we were unrecognisable, and you couldn't tell the colour of the car or the passengers, we were very happy. I wouldn't say the experience had been fun, but once again we had proved that the promises of God never fail. I never did see a tractor around there again.

Did you know angels can drive a tractor or truck? These drivers can change a tyre on a Land Rover in record time. I can't count how many times after travelling for hours without seeing another vehicle we'd have a puncture or a blowout and within the time to send up a quick SOS message to Father, along would come a truck. They never passed by without stopping and in minutes the wheel was off and the spare in place. Special AA angels, I guess!

I had similar experiences when I accidentally locked the keys inside the Land Rover – disconcerting, though easily done. In those cases, money was usually involved as they debated who would open the door for the least amount of money. Maybe they weren't the usual sort of angels!

Margaret Davies served in Guinea-Bissau from 1986–2004 in both midwifery and evangelism roles. Since her return home she has lived in South Wales.

IT NEVER RAINED ON THURSDAYS

Matt and Margaret Paton

Many years ago, we worked in a small town in the centre of France. The place where we held our Gospel meetings was not available anymore and we hunted for another one. Matt went to a meeting in another town one evening and a young man who had been delivered from drugs came to him and said, 'You must look for a house you need and say, "Lord give me the money to buy it!"' We felt this was a word from Heaven, even though we laughed at first over it. The only house we could find was a 400-year-old one, empty, and in desperate need of much work to do on it. We visited the mayor of the town who had the key and when he showed it to us, he said: 'Some people go to America for adventure, but to do up an old place like this ... that is adventure!' He said he would go before us to break the cobwebs which looked like curtains in the whole place! However, it was for sale and as our field leaders of that time came to see it, they agreed it was just right; but we had no money. It was very cheap and so we began to pray every evening till 1:00 a.m. for over a month. Then at that time, though not having made any requests for money, a gift to cover the buying of this old house came through!

Later on, we needed to change the dangerous roof. Workmen came for three weeks, but on weekends they would put a weather-proof cover on the unfinished roof. We told them not to waste their time doing that as we had prayed it would not rain for three weeks – but their faith did not go that far, and they put the cover on, nevertheless. But the Lord kept off the rain till the roof was finished! Matt set to work to clean and alter it so that we could live upstairs with our two little boys and use the downstairs for meetings. It had a toilet in the courtyard which was a hole in the ground and one cold tap for the whole building (no bathroom of course). Despite these things, it was ideal, and we were very happy.

But the children's meetings had to be held in the open-air meeting on Thursdays which at that time was the day all children in France had off from school. We went on to the town market square and had around forty children each week. We had prayed much about the weather, and during those six months of summer it didn't rain at all on Thursdays. However, the government changed the school day off to Wednesday and we said to the children: 'We will see you on Wednesday next week and it MAY rain on Thursday' – which it did!

We then moved into this old house and had the meetings there. These included gatherings for young people who seemed to love the place and came at all hours of the day (especially at mealtimes). There is one incident with these young people which none of them will ever forget. Matt was speaking to them one day and said how they must be ready to meet the Lord as nobody knows if they will be here tomorrow. They laughed a bit at this but that night one of them was walking to the next village having drunk too much, and a lorry which could not see him in the dark knocked him down and killed him. Those young people came back to tell us, and were white-faced and much touched by what had been said only the day before.

We were in this house for six years of great joy, and then handed the whole work over to a French pastor who passed the group of believers to another pastor after a few years and so the work went on. Around 2015, we were asked to take a mission there for the forty years of witness in the town.

It was a great, moving time – and marvellous to see that same building, now much improved, still used for the proclamation of the Gospel. It was wonderful to see the church now turned into a great tool to bless Gannat (Food Bank and other efforts). We visited the town and found so much of it had been modernised, and most of those children and young people had moved away to find work. But surely they will never forget the miracles and blessings of those long-ago days.

Matt and Margaret Paton have served in France from 1964 till the present day, making them perhaps the longest serving UK WEC missionaries still overseas. They have been involved in evangelism and church planting in as many as sixteen different places, including Gannat, Clermont-Ferrand and Roubaix.

HOSPITALITY

Hazel Wallis

It was May, the time for the annual church assembly in Guinea-Bissau. I was living with an African pastor and his family on language study and orientation on the island of Bolama. There was a boat twice a week to Bissau, but this weekend it hadn't arrived, so we set off to go overland – 'we' being Pastor Quintino and his wife, Inacia, me and a friend Loida with her nine-month-old baby. The journey began with a small boat ferry to Sao Joao on the mainland, where we walked for a while and then caught a passing vehicle that took us to a crossroads. After an hour and half's wait, we caught a public transport bus to the town of Enxude, where the ferry went to Bissau once a day on the tide. We arrived at the port to be told we had missed it by fifteen minutes.

So, no help for it but to bed down in a covered space there overnight with everyone. We were soon joined by another group from Catio with Pastor Paulo making their way to the assembly. Paulo had some rice they were taking to Bissau and we had some tomatoes. All we needed to cook a meal was a saucepan. Inacia said, 'Let's go and ask in the nearest house.' I went with her.

At the first house, maybe a quarter of a mile away, Inacia simply asked the lady of the house if we could borrow a saucepan. At which the lady sat us down, offered us a bowl of rice and some mangoes, sent her daughter to fetch water at the well quite a long way away, relit her own fire, took our rice and cleaned it and then cooked our rice and tomatoes. She sent us on our way with food and water. All this to two complete strangers who weren't her tribe and couldn't even speak her language. The lady was Balanta and Inacia is Papel, and I of course am English. We prayed God's blessing on that dear lady!

That evening we went into the village and had an open-air meeting and preached the Gospel – there weren't any Christians in the village then.

Years later, the church in Bubaque had a new Balanta pastor from Enxude and I was telling him this story. He said, 'That was my house!' The Lord had truly blessed the family: the lady had come to faith and her son was serving the Lord!

Hazel Wallis served from 1983–2009 in Guinea-Bissau, on the Bijagós Islands.

15

CAKE IN THE CONGO

Margaret White

My friend and colleague Annette wasn't a flamboyant character. She was easily pleased and didn't ask for much in life. A steady, consistent worker, who quietly got on with doing whatever was needed. No fuss. However, on her birthday, she DID like the occasion to be marked with a cake.

No need for anything else. Just a cake. There were no shops, so usually I would see that a cake was made. No big deal.

One year, as Annette's birthday drew near, all our chickens died of fowl pest. Not just ours. Fowl pest is very contagious. All the neighbours' chickens died too. Nobody had eggs to sell, and all my cake recipes needed eggs.

Our school started each day with a time of singing, Bible reading and prayers with our form classes. The boys prayed about all sorts of things. I shared that I couldn't fulfil our custom of a birthday cake for Annette because I lacked eggs. They saw it as important, but couldn't help, because their chickens had died too. But they asked the Lord to send me some eggs to make a cake!

Later that day, I had a visitor who had walked in from a village fifteen kilometres away. She said,

'I was pounding the first fruits of my rice crop, and thought I'd give it to you this time.' And she handed me a bowl of freshly pounded rice, with the customary two eggs nestled on top. 'Thank you, Mama!'

I told her why her gift was so special that day and we praised the Lord together.

The cake was made. 'Thank You, Father!'

Margaret White served in Zaïre (now the Democratic Republic of Congo) from 1970–1996, first in the secondary school to help young Christians enter the professions, and then travelling to the village churches for discipleship and mission awareness seminars. On returning to the UK, she continued to serve God in her home-town of Coatbridge, near Glasgow.

GOD ANSWERS PRAYER

Pat Urquhart

One time when we lived and worked in Malba, a Birifor village in Burkina Faso, we had been home to visit my mother – the only grandparent our boys knew. We were able to take the month's annual leave to visit her in Scotland. On our return, it was the time when the millet and maize crops were nearly ready for harvest. When we got out to the village, everywhere was cultivated and the tall maize and millet was growing everywhere. This was the norm and we were used to it.

However, it was always a problem as all available space was used to grow crops and there was no room to hold the heathen funerals. Everywhere in the village of Malba and its surroundings had been cultivated except a bit of land that was right next door to the mission property. Our kitchen window looked out on it!

When we arrived back, it was to discover that a funeral was taking place there. These funerals went on for sometimes three days and nights and were accompanied by all the usual wailing, mourning, dancing, sacrifices, drums, etc. – all very noisy and very disturbing. It made sleep impossible. Our boys were about ten and seven at the time (if we remember properly) – not the best re-entry to Birifor land! The second night was as bad as the first, very hard to sleep and very hard to settle back into our home.

The morning after the second night when I was having my quiet time with the Lord, my Psalm for the day was Psalm 125, and verse 3 stood out to me:

'The sceptre of the wicked will not remain over the land allotted to the righteous ...'

So, I said to the family when we had breakfast together that the Lord was going to do something about the funerals. I shared the verse, and we discussed its meaning and the implications. We then committed it again to the Lord.

Later on in the morning, we had a visit from Sie Dah. He was a believer but lived in the extended family home with his wife and children. He had been praying about acquiring a piece of land so he could build his own house and not have to pass the family idols when entering and leaving where they lived. We'd been praying for that with him at the church prayer meeting for some time. He came that morning, to tell us good news! He had managed to buy a bit of land. We rejoiced with him!

'Where is it?' we asked him.

'Oh', he said, 'it's that piece of land right next door to you!'

So, there were no more funerals on that bit of land, and we had Sie Dah as our neighbour. Isn't the Lord good? AND faithful to His Word.

Wilf and Pat Urquhart, from Scotland, worked amongst the Birifor people in Burkina Faso from 1972–1991 and helped build up the church in the village of Malba, which is now sending out its own missionaries.

A CLOSE WALK WITH GOD

Wilf Urquhart

Part One

The Birifor church in the village of Malba was a very 'go ahead' church and was often seeking new ways of sharing the Gospel in and around the village. They had regular visits to the local weekly markets to share the Gospel and several surrounding villages were also visited. The mid-week prayer meeting was well attended, and a good spirit of prayer was evident. Prayer was made for all branches of the work and sometimes we ran short on time as so many wanted to take part.

One day, we were asked by members of the church in the village if it would be possible to have an extra prayer meeting. Our reply was to say, 'What's wrong with the prayer meeting you already have?' They responded, 'There's nothing wrong with it, but we would like this new one to be solely for outreach prayer.' When asked when they would like this new prayer meeting to take place, they responded by saying, '5:00 a.m. Monday mornings.' We were somewhat taken by surprise by the day they suggested as it followed on after a full day of Sunday activities. Their reasoning was that it would be easy to remember Monday as it followed close on Sunday.

Arrangements were duly made, and we prepared the church pressure lamp and fired it up on Monday morning. It was strange walking up to the church from our house in the total darkness as there was nobody about at that hour. On arrival at the church I noticed Aline, an elderly Christian lady, sitting on the doorstep waiting to get in. I greeted her and opened the door, and we went in and awaited the others. Shortly after five we had quite a gathering of the core members of the church. It was a good meeting and the prayers that were made were fervent, seeking the Lord's blessing on the church and particularly on the outreach and casual attenders of whom there were quite a few. A little before 7:00 a.m., we closed the meeting and all went home to get on with their own work both in the home and in the fields.

This meeting went on week by week and every time I arrived at the church door at 5:00 a.m. on Monday morning, there was Aline sitting waiting to get in. I was amazed, as Aline was a typical woman from the bush and had neither watch nor alarm clock in her home. It amazed me that she was always there before I arrived with the lamp. One day I asked her how she managed to be there on time every Monday.

'Oh, it's really quite easy,' she said.

'Please tell me,' I replied, 'as I don't find it easy and need an alarm clock to waken me up.'

Her reply astonished me: 'When I go to bed on Sunday night, I ask the Lord to waken me up in time for the prayer meeting and He always does.'

This somewhat puzzled me so I asked her: 'What if you were wakened in the night by a noise or disturbance, would you think that it was time to get up?'

'No,' she replied. 'I asked the Lord to waken me in time for the meeting, so if I'm wakened I know that it's time to get up.' Wow! I thought. What a close walk this woman has with the Lord! I wish I could emulate her in this very practical way.

We sometimes think that these people who have lived all their days in the shadow of Animism can never enjoy a close and intimate walk with the Lord. How wrong we can be! This woman who, at the time, could neither read nor write could nonetheless enjoy such a close walk with God. She asked God to do something for her and she fully believed that He would do it. Is my relationship with God as close and intimate as that?

Part Two

Aline was heading out the door of her house to go to the church for an evening service. As she was stepping out, she saw a snake slither rapidly into her house through the open door. She chased after it but after an extensive hunt was unable to find it. Not being able to do anything more about it she closed the door and went to church. When the pastor asked if anyone needed prayer, Aline explained what had happened at her house with the snake. The pastor prayed for her and asked the Lord to close the snake's mouth so that it couldn't bite Aline when she went into the house. As he was praying, he brought his thumb and forefinger together indicating that this is what would happen to the snake. It would be unable to bite. He also asked the Lord that He would take any fear away from Aline and that she would not be afraid to lie down on her mat and go to sleep.

Aline went home after the prayer meeting and opened the door of her house but there was no sign of the snake. So, remembering what the pastor prayed she went in and lay down on her mat and went to sleep. She slept very well that night.

In the morning my wife, Pat, went over to Aline's house to enquire after her well-being. When Aline came out of the house, she said to Pat, 'What are you doing here, you should be teaching your children?'

Pat asked her, 'Did you sleep well last night?'

Aline replied, 'Never better!'

Pat responded, 'Weren't you frightened to lie down on your mat knowing that the snake was still in your house? Weren't you frightened that it would bite you during the night?'

'Why would I be frightened?' responded Aline. 'Didn't the pastor pray that the snake's mouth would be closed and that it wouldn't be able to bite me?' When she said that she did with her thumb and forefinger exactly what the pastor had done. She then said, 'The snake couldn't bite me because God had closed its mouth, so why would I be afraid? Why would I be frightened to lie down on my mat and go to sleep? Wasn't God there with me so there was no need for me to be afraid because He had closed the snake's mouth?'

I wonder how well I would have slept in that house knowing that there was a snake on the loose. I wonder if I could display such faith and trust in God. It was both a blessing and a challenge to live alongside people who had such a down-to-earth trust in God.

Aline is now a senior member of the church and her life is an example to the younger ones who are growing up in the congregation. The church could use many more of the calibre of Aline. We who go out as missionaries to people groups like the Birifors of Burkina Faso sometimes meet people of this special spiritual calibre and they are a shining example to us of the Lord at work within His people. May He be so obviously at work within us as well.

Wilf and Pat Urquhart, from Perth in Scotland, worked amongst the Birifor people in Burkina Faso from 1972–1991 and helped build up the church in the village of Malba which is now sending out its own missionaries. After returning home, they were the WEC Regional Co-ordinators for Scotland for many years, organising the annual 'Highlands and Islands tour' for new WEC recruits and missionaries home on furlough.

OLYMPICS

Mavis Rodger

Ask and you will receive. **Luke 11:10**

Two of us from the WEC Youth Department at the WEC headquarters, Bulstrode, were assigned to go to the 1976 Montreal Olympic Outreach with Youth With A Mission. We had to pray in the money for our fares. Before going to Montreal, I was also going to East Germany. As the sum of these trips involved quite a lot of money, it was a bit overwhelming.

Every morning, we used to attend the chapel service in Bulstrode before we started work. Shortly before I went to Germany, Peter Plummer, the Manager of Bulstrode, spoke in the meeting. In the course of his talk he said, 'If you need to get alone with God, never mind where you work for once. Just spend time with God.' That registered with me. The next afternoon, I decided to go to my room, which was on the mezzanine floor, and pray specifically for money for Montreal.

Kneeling beside my bed I prayed aloud, 'Lord, I need money for Montreal this week ...' No sooner had I uttered those words, when ... slowly ... slowly ... coming under the gap in the door ... was an envelope. On it were the Olympic rings and inside was a gift of money. 'Well Lord, I didn't mean right this minute!'

The person, who was so sensitive to the Holy Spirit and His promptings, remains unknown, but it was certainly very encouraging (I didn't spend long out of the office either!).

John and Mavis Rodger were Long Term workers making Short Term practical mission trips to various countries on different continents from 1979 to 2002. Since John passed away, Mavis continues to live in Kilcreggan, over the Clyde from Glasgow.

POLITICIAN TO PASTOR

Heather Donnelly

When I lived in a small village in Senegal – helping with a small clinic, holding meetings, having sewing classes with boys and girls – there was one young man who really stood out from the rest. It was not because of his stature or high intelligence, but because of certain qualities that were recognised by his friends – so much so that they called him 'Politician'!

He worked hard at school and when he came to take some tests to see if he could go on to Secondary School, which would have meant that he would have to leave his village, he was really excited. I was sure he would pass and continued to pray for him. He had been one of the first in the village to become a Christian and had already known some persecution. He had also been ridiculed because he would walk down paths forbidden by the village as they were supposedly controlled by the spirits.

The results of the test became known and his name was not on the list of those who had passed.

He came and told us, and we encouraged him to look again carefully at the list. But no, his name was not there, and he was devastated. Later it was discovered that a parent in the village had bribed the Headmaster to put the name of his son on the list, but he had not passed the test. So the one who was then left off the list to keep the numbers correct was our friend the 'Politician.'

After much thought and prayer, he decided to leave the village and go to the nearest town about thirty kilometres away. He was able to live with extended family members and worked in the fields for them and others, to gain some money. He then took extra classes and studied really hard. He kept his money in a box under his bed. After more exams, which he finally passed, he was ready to start at Secondary School. But, oh dear – he went to his box under the bed and it was empty! Someone had stolen his money. He came back to our village and came to tell us. We could see he was so upset. We prayed with him, and he knew God would provide for him and his future. He did very well in his studies and grew in his own spiritual life and his involvement with the local Christian group.

The years have passed and now there are about a hundred believers in his village. And who is the Pastor? The 'Politician'! God is so faithful, and He watches over His loved ones.

Heather Donnelly served in Senegal, 1969–78, in a variety of roles including medical work, teaching in the agricultural Bible school and in youth/children's work. Thereafter, she served at the UK WEC headquarters.

20

THE FAITH OF NON-CHRISTIANS

Sue Frampton

After about a year of living in Kpassa in northern Ghana where we were trying to learn Konkomba, we were frustrated. Since Kpassa was a market town, most people spoke in Twi, the trade-language, even if they were Konkomba. There were also several dialects of Konkomba an_d we were trying to learn a particular dialect, Likpakpaln. We decided to move into a village which was 100 per cent Konkomba where everyone used Likpakpaln.

We visited a village and asked the chief if we could stay there for a time and we were generously given two mud rooms in a compound owned by two brothers who lived there with several wives and about twenty children. We lived very simply and spent most of our time in the open area of the compound or out in the village chatting with the people. Our language skills improved quickly.

This village was on top of a hill, and the river where the women fetched water from was in the valley. Since it was nearing the end of the dry season, the river was running low and was very polluted. The people in the compound where we lived, knowing we were Christians, asked us to pray for rain which, of course, we did. There had been no sign at all of rain until this time. Before they went to bed that night, they put all their bowls and buckets under the eaves of their roof, ready to catch the rain they were expecting. We were amazed at their faith since they still knew nothing of the Truth. Half-way through the night the heavens opened, and it poured! All their utensils were filled in no time.

Later, when we were more proficient in the language, we returned to this village for a series of evangelistic meetings and, before long, the majority of the village had turned to the Lord. The church continued to do well there after that, and we visited regularly.

Sue and her husband David were in Ghana from 1987–1997. They were in the north, church planting among the Konkomba people. Later on they served in the Middle East. Back in the UK, both Sue and David took 'active retirement' status in WEC, with the emphasis on 'active'!

21

ANSWERED PRAYER

Jackie Rowe

Forty years ago, I was working as a midwife in a walled city in the Middle East. We were a small team of medical workers staffing a hospital which served people in an extremely wide area. One free day, Kathy and I decided to visit a woman who had recently had her baby in the hospital. We knew that Shutt lay to the north of the town, so we pointed the Land Rover northwards and set off across the plain on deeply rutted tracks. The golden bleakness of the landscape was broken up by villages every few miles, each with their surrounding irrigated and cultivated fields.

We came to a fork in the track and took the right-hand exit. Half a mile later I pulled up at a petrol station – one rickety pump beside a small shack – to ask if we were still on the right road. 'Yes, just keep in the valley between those two mountains and you will soon be there.'

We entered the village, with the cemetery on our left, and manoeuvred the Land Rover between the tall, mud houses which looked like brown layer cakes. We parked in the square, open space in the centre of Shutt. A woman sitting in her doorway peered at us speculatively as we approached, picking our way through chickens and children, passing the cakes of cow-dung drying in the sun. 'Peace be upon you.' 'And upon you be peace.' The age-old greetings seemed perfectly to fit the scene. 'We're looking for Aisha bint Ahmed – can you direct us to her house?' An older woman suddenly appeared from the shadows and took control. 'Yes, yes, I'll take you, follow me.'

As we strolled through the village, our entourage swelled as other women and children joined us. We learned that all the able-bodied men and women were out working – either in the fields or collecting firewood or caring for the sheep and goats. We came to the house, a poor two-storeyed affair. As we stepped from the courtyard into the house, the pungent smell of animal waste wafted from an open door. The ground floor is always home for the animals in that part of the world. We paused so that our eyes could adjust to the unlighted gloom and then followed our guide up the winding mud staircase to the living quarters. It was obviously one of the poorer homes, but even so our welcome was royal. We left our shoes outside the door and stepped into the room which served as living-room and bedroom for all the family.

We were escorted to the place of honour at the far end of the room and sat down on the thin, grubby mattress there. The only furnishings the room boasted were similar mattresses all the way round the edge of the room, and some scruffy, hard pillows against the walls. We leaned back on our pillows and watched as the room filled up with jostling, excited women and children.

A young mother next to me breast-fed her baby, unmoved by the flies carpeting the youngster's sticky eyes. Our hostess brought in a flask of tea and a tray of small handleless cups. Again and again our cups were filled and, hot and thirsty from the journey in the afternoon sun, we welcomed the scalding liquid.

As we talked, I realised that the conversation revolved around one main topic – RAIN – or rather, the lack of it. In that village they had not had rain for over two years and the well had run dry. Even though we'd had rain in the town, not so very far away, this place was parched and dusty and crying out for water. For their own basic need for drinking, cooking and washing they had to buy a tank of water each day from the town. Meanwhile, their fields were slowing turning to dust.

Suddenly, above the chatter, I was aware that the Lord was speaking to me. I turned to Kathy and said, 'I believe the Lord wants us to pray for rain for these people. Will you agree in your heart as I pray?' She nodded. I raised my voice: 'Listen everybody. Our Lord is the Lord Jesus Christ, and we believe that as we pray in His name, God hears and answers. Would you like us to pray in His name for rain for your village?' A startled silence was followed by a chorus of assent, even a grey-bearded old man who stood in the doorway seemed to agree. I continued, 'When you pray you wash with water. I am not going to wash now, because we believe that the most important thing is to have a clean heart. My heart is clean because Jesus died on the cross and took the punishment for my sins. He rose again from the dead and is alive now. That is why I can pray in His name.'

Even the children were quiet by now as I lifted my hands and prayed very simply. 'Lord God, please send rain to this place, in the name of the Lord Jesus Christ.' There were a few heartfelt 'Amens' and then we all began to leave. We were taken to another, taller, house and from the flat roof we could see the cracked, dry earth circumscribing the village. The cloudless blue sky seemed empty of promise.

Six days later, it began to rain in the town. As Kathy and I walked to the hospital in the tropical downpour we both looked to the north. The black clouds seemed just as dense over there too … 'Thank You, Lord.'

Next day, we once more set off along the rutted roads. Several inches of rain had fallen the previous day and sometimes we had to navigate deep pot-holes full of water. We parked in the same place in Shutt, but as we stepped out a young woman was hurrying towards us. 'Come with me, you must see what has happened.' Once again, the crowd gathered as we processed through the narrow alleys between the towering houses. We ascended again to the now-familiar flat roof. Again, we viewed the panorama before us. Where there had been white, cracked, sun-hardened soil, we now saw brown earth smiling at us from scores of fields. The rain had come and the whole place seemed to shine with happiness. The name of Jesus had been glorified in that Muslim village.

Jackie Rowe worked as a midwife in the Middle East from 1974–81. Throughout the '90s, she frequently re-visited the area.

22

EU NÃO ME SINTO SÓ/
I DO NOT FEEL ALONE

Amy Cuthbert

September 1983

We had decided that Jayne and Judith could start in BCS (Bourofaye Christian School for missionaries' children). Jayne was eight-and-a-half and Judith was seven. They were both keen to go as their friends, the Goodman girls, were there – but I knew that they had no idea what being away from home for weeks without seeing us meant. Robert was due to start home school and I knew I could not cope with three children at different ages in schooling. I had never thought of them going until secondary school age, but it seemed the right thing to do.

During the months before, as I wrestled with the idea of them being away, I studied the lives of mothers in the Bible who had had to part with their children at a young age ...

Jochebed parted with Moses when he was seven years old. He was to go into a pagan palace and learn all the culture of the Egyptians. But Jochebed had taught him enough so that he made the right choice when the time came and 'chose rather to suffer affliction with the people of God' (Heb. 11:25).

Hannah had kept Samuel at home for the first few years and then, when he went to live with Eli in the temple, he was able to hear and then know the voice of God and obey Him. I prayed that the input I was having into the lives of Jayne and Judith would also prove to be fruitful for the Kingdom of God. What a privilege I had had for three and a half years to home-school them and, alongside the local children, teach them the stories of the Bible. But I wanted a definite sign that God was able to speak directly into their young hearts.

Jayne had asked Jesus to be her Saviour earlier – but Judith not yet. We were in Bissau the night before they were to go to school, and I was reading a Scripture Union story to them. The boy (Gus) in the story had done something naughty and asked forgiveness of God. It was similar to something Judith had just done and she piped up, 'I want to be like Gus and ask God to forgive me.' We prayed and she received Christ as Saviour. It was of God – I had not in any way orchestrated it. God gave me the assurance I was seeking. But we were leaving our little ones in another country. It was a day's journey from Bissau – and our home was six hours by boat from Bissau. There was no way we could get there in an emergency. And communication was slow to non-existent.

The next morning, we were leaving at 6:30 a.m. for the day's journey to Senegal. In my quiet time, God spoke to me through Psalm 112 verses 7-8: 'The righteous shall have no fear of bad news; his heart is steadfast trusting in the Lord.' As we and the Goodman family headed off, everyone on the compound was there to pray with us and see us off. A new chorus was being learned and the children sang loudly all the way: 'Eu não me sinto só' – 'I do not feel alone because the angel of the Lord is with me, camping around me, defending me.' The children sang and the mothers cried!

We got them settled into school and made painful good-byes. To cry or not to cry? Some said it unsettled the children if they saw us crying. Others, that if we didn't show some emotion, they would feel unloved. I'm sure I cried!

We had an overnight stop in Ziguinchor and then left for Bissau the next morning. The first hurdle was to cross the border, knowing that to return we needed visas and permits for the car to cross. This paperwork could take days back in Bissau. We had a few days in Bissau waiting for a boat and I spent the time pacing the floor of the apartment. My heart was in turmoil. Others were concerned for my emotional well-being. I couldn't speak about my trauma or I would have gone to pieces.

By the weekend, we then had to take the six-hour boat journey to Bubaque, putting more distance between us and the girls. There was no way back. And then home to a quieter house. Robert and Susan missed their older sisters. We missed their lively presence in the house. And we would not hear from them for weeks.

So – to start home-schooling with Robert. I didn't have the mental energy to do it. Early November, we had our first mid-term break with Jayne and Judith. They were getting on well in BCS. Judith had cried the first few nights, but Linda (Williamson) got into bed beside her until she went to sleep.

After mid-term, Hazel Wallis had come to Bubaque for a few months for orientation and we were going to Uno island for Norman to work on the gardens. We stayed in Angodigo – one small room behind the church building. I had books with me to do school with Robert, but there was no way I could get myself together. We lived on the verandah during the day and there were always groups of children wanting to play with Robert and Susan. I discovered Robert giving away T-shirts one day in exchange for a ride on a cow! The young herdsmen rode the cows back to the village in the evenings. Then Robert and Susan got covered in ticks! Hazel and I spent hours extracting them without leaving the heads in. We had to coax them to reverse out of their skin – I think with paraffin. Anyway, it worked, and the children were none the worse.

In all the years our children were in BCS we had 'no report of bad news'!

Amy Cuthbert, with her husband Norman, served in Guinea-Bissau 1975–1991. On returning home, they were WEC Co-ordinators for Ireland 1992–1999; UK Deputies & HQ Managers 1999–2007; Directors for all Ireland 2007–2016. Their various offspring have continued in the missionary tradition.

PROVIDENCE

The Lord Himself goes before you
(Deut. 18:10)

LOST IN TRANSLATION

Dave Northcote

It was my first encounter with an International incident within a police state. A country renowned for its order and lack of public protests was suddenly encouraged to protest by the heads of government. Students rioted while uniformed police turned a blind eye. What on earth was going on?

My foray into the streets only confirmed what I suspected. The offending nation was not British, but there was no way the locals would attempt to make a distinction between the Brits and the nationals responsible for this outrageous breach of their security. Faces normally familiar to me had taken on a sinister glare and obscenities new to me seemed to fall about my ears. Spitting was a common enough occurrence but never usually directed at a fellow human being.

Shortly after returning to my flat, one female and four male police officers were knocking on my door. Looking through the spy hole, I recognised the lady and one of the men and so I invited them in, offering tea and fruit as is the custom. They seemed congenial enough but the long and short of it was they were concerned for my safety and were putting me under house arrest until further notice. As they were leaving, I said what any grateful Brit would say to the Bobby on the beat, 'Thank you for warning me.' No sooner had these words dropped from my lips than the expressions on the officers' faces turned truly hostile.

They had left me with a quandary; I must have misunderstood something, but what was it? What could I do about it since I couldn't get my re-entry visas, my citizen's permit, my business licence or any other legal document without their approval? I called up a Christian student I'd been mentoring and invited him over. When he arrived, it was noticeable that even he seemed cool towards me. But when I explained what had happened, he was quick to point out that what I had said to those police officers as they were leaving implied that they were mere servants sent for my benefit!

Not for the first time, I applied James 1:5: 'If any of you lacks wisdom, you should ask God, who gives generously to all without finding fault, and it will be given to you.' I discussed the possibility of a remedy with this Christian student and he agreed to produce a hand-written letter with my sentiments but worded appropriately in his culture to the Chief of Police.

The next day, I set off in a downpour on my bike with the letter safely tucked away under my cape. When I arrived at the Police headquarters, the lady police officer who had come to my flat was by the reception. I asked to speak with the Chief of Police and was curtly told he was out. I said I had an important letter for him, and I would await his return. When he arrived, I threw out my hand in a gesture of friendship that was instantly rebuffed. The policewoman intervened and handed him my letter which he sat down to read. As his eyes settled on the last full stop a gleam came into them and he leapt to his feet and pumped my hand!

A couple of days later, another police officer came to my flat and asked me for a passport photo, the purpose for which remained a mystery. He seemed happy with the one I produced and left. It was shortly after this I received a phone call from the police lady inviting me to the Police station, but again, the explanation was one that I couldn't comprehend.

Upon arrival I was ushered into what must normally be used as a boardroom where the horse-shoe table was bedecked with fancy nibbles and various refreshments. As I surveyed the room, it dawned on me that I had been lumped together with five overseas nationals in business suits. One of the senior officers began his speech commending the six of us for ...? But again, this was lost in translation. One by one, we were presented with a signed document in a presentation case and a plastic ID badge complete with passport photo and the city police insignia. Underneath were the words 'Foreign Business Liaison Officer for ... Police.' I was told that if I knew of any foreign businessman experiencing difficulty with legal responsibilities, I had direct access to the Chief of Police to explain and rectify the difficulty ...

'I can do all this through Him who gives me strength' (Phil. 4:13) ... surely I knew not the half!

Dave and Becky Northcote served in the Far East 1993–2005. Dave was deputy branch leader for eight years before returning to the UK where he now has a role co-ordinating the care of many of the contributors of this publication.

24

SAMUEL'S STORY

Wilf Urquhart

'Kuunpé' lived in a village close to the Burkina Faso border with Ghana. His heathen name 'Kuunpé' means literally 'death has entered,' and was the name given to children whose mothers died in giving them birth. He was married with two wives and had quite a large family. He followed the way of his own people who were animists. He was dissatisfied with his own way of life but had no idea either how to improve it or where to look for betterment. One night, he had a dream which greatly exercised and troubled him. Here is the dream and its amazing outcome ...

In his dream, he was told to go over the border into Ghana to the town of Tuna, which was close to the border with his own country. On entering the market on the fringe of the town, he would see a white man speaking to a gathering of people. This man would have 'something' in his hand and would keep referring to it and then, lifting his head he would speak more to the gathering. This would be repeated numerous times. He was to speak to this man and do what he told him. When he got up in the morning, he shared what had happened in the night. His family encouraged him to go and 'check it out' as it might be important for them all.

Preparations were made and Kuunpé set out for the border and the village of Tuna. On arrival at the edge of the village, he discovered a crowd of people listening to a white man. As Kuunpé listened to him, he noticed that he had something in his hand, and he kept referring to it and then speaking more to the crowd. This is just what had been shown to him in his dream and he was amazed. This caused him to stick around and listen to what was being shared.

He was struck by the message that the white man was sharing, and it began to warm his heart.

He wondered if this was what he had been looking for but had not discovered in his own animistic religion. The more he listened, the more he was captivated by this man's message. The message concerned a God who loved mankind so much that He sent His Son to die on a cross to atone for the sin of the world. Kuunpé had never heard about such a God but as the story developed, he was more and more drawn towards this man and this God. When the talk drew to a close, Kuunpé went up to him and thanked him for what he had shared. The man, Eric Christie, working with WEC International, had lived and worked in Tuna for many years. He regularly went to the weekly market and shared God's Word with all who would listen.

When Kuunpé spoke to Eric, a bond seemed to grow between them and Eric invited him to come to his home and hear more about this God 'who so loved the world that He gave His only begotten Son that whosoever believed in Him should not perish but should have everlasting life.' Kuunpé went with Eric and discovered that he had quite a few others staying with him as well and that they were daily studying the Bible and being taught the Christian way. All that Kuunpé heard from Eric warmed his heart and one day he surrendered his life to 'Eric's God' and his life was deeply changed. With the daily teaching from God's Word, Kuunpé grew in his faith and came into a deep relationship with God. It was no longer Eric's God but rather his own God and Saviour. During those six months, Kuunpé decided that he could no longer be called by this name, Kuunpé, and decided, with Eric's help, to choose a name from the Bible. The name that really pleased him was Samuel and from that day onwards he took that name.

Having spent some six months with Eric, he had another dream. He felt that God was challenging him in his dream to go back over the border to his own people and to share with them all that he had learnt in this little Bible School. He shared this with Eric, who heartily agreed with him and encouraged him to go back to Gangalama, his village in Burkina Faso. Samuel went home and shared with his own family and village all that had happened to him in Tuna. His own people were amazed at the change in him and were greatly attracted by the message that he was sharing. God started to work firstly in Gangalama and then in some surrounding villages, and many people came and listened to Samuel's amazing story. People began surrendering their lives to Christ and quite a number of people began gathering together to worship God and to listen to His Word.

The work was growing so quickly that Samuel realised that he needed help. He was a very young Christian himself and wasn't very clear how to set up a church. He knew that there was another town not too far from his village in Burkina Faso and that there were white people there and they had a church. So, one day, he sent his oldest son Jacob to Batié to invite these white people to come to his village. We were amazed at what this young man told us, so we arranged a day when we would go to Gangalama along with some of the elders from the local church.

On arrival we were amazed at what we saw. There was a large crowd waiting and they were eager to hear from their visitors. When we heard Samuel's story, we were totally amazed at what God was doing. These new believers had come up with answers to questions that had perplexed the church in Burkina Faso for many years. They had decided that a Christian could not marry an unbeliever because light could not live with darkness. They had decided that church attendance on Sunday was a 'must' for all believers and that Sunday was to be 'set aside' for God. These were questions that had dogged the church for many years and these new believers had come up with 'God inspired' answers. Wow! All without input from foreign missionaries. Isn't God amazing?

From that day forward, the church in Batié sent someone to take regular services in Gangalama. The work grew and soon other villages were 'buying into' this new message and churches were being set up. When you consider that all this sprang from a dream, it brings you up short and you see dreams in a new light. God uses so many different ways of reaching out with the Good News of the Gospel. We just need to be walking in close fellowship with our Lord and be open and aware of what He is doing in our world. After all, who would consider setting up a new pioneer work through a dream!

These churches in the Gangalama area have now given some choice young people for full-time training for God's work and some of these are now in the work full-time as pastors. Isn't it so thrilling to see how God lets His message reach out to those who are still waiting to hear? He is truly a God who loves 'the whole world.' Praise His name!

Wilf and Pat Urquhart, from Perth in Scotland, worked amongst the Birifor people in Burkina Faso from 1972–1991. Serving as WEC Regional Co-ordinators for Scotland after their return home, they became well-known across the length and breadth of Scotland and are still asked to stand in for church ministers who are away on holiday.

25

GOD SPEAKS TODAY
THROUGH DREAMS

Paul M. Harvey

Just like in the Bible, both Old and New Testaments, God speaks today through dreams. I know this through personal experience. Here is an account of two dreams which I have no doubt came from God – one was given for guidance, the other for comfort at a difficult time.

The first dream took place when I was twenty-four. I had been a Christian for two years, had recently finished my teacher training course and was working in a multicultural Middle School (8-12 age range) in Slough, UK.

One night I was sleeping on a hard, wooden church floor – I was on a weekend away with a charity group and the other volunteers were spread out in their sleeping bags around the hall. I woke up in the middle of the night having had the clearest of dreams. Though the content of the dream could have left me unsettled, I was convinced it came from God because of the overwhelming sense of peace and assurance that accompanied it.

In the dream I was in a dilapidated, crumbling-down city, possibly in Latin America, and a hurricane was raging all around. Blocks of masonry were falling, the wind was howling ... but we were safe. With me was a group of about ten children and we were huddled against a wall in what used to be a room before the roof had been blown off. I could see out through what used to be the door into the street where a solitary child was standing. He was dressed in a tatty T-shirt and shorts, and his hair was being tossed by the raging wind.

'Go and bring the child in,' I heard a voice say.

'But it's too dangerous,' I replied.

'All you need to do is say "yes" and you'll be fine. Will you go?'

'Yes,' I said, knowing I'd be able to bring the child back to the safety of the group.

I woke up to the quietness of the church hall. The others were still asleep. As I went over the dream in my mind, it came to me that God was calling me to a life of Christian service. Teaching in a school in Slough was just the start – a stepping-stone towards something else. That dream, in the summer of 1984, was my initial call to full-time missionary work.

Twelve years later, I had the second dream which I consider to be a direct word from God. In the intervening time I had met and married my wife Rose, we had attended Bible College, worked in a UK church and arrived in Spain as members of the missionary organization WEC International. It wasn't Latin America as in the dream, but it *was* a Spanish-speaking country. And there was a strong Latin American element involved – before we met, Rose had circumnavigated Latin America on the ship M/V Doulos. Furthermore, despite its Christian heritage, Spain was a land in desperate need of the Good News of Jesus.

After four years in Spain, one day I received a telephone call. My father, who with my mother had emigrated from the UK to Australia twelve years before, was ill in hospital. It crossed my mind to jump on a plane to make the trip out there, but on the other hand I had no reason to believe his illness was that serious. And then I had the dream …

… I picked up the telephone and dialled the number of a friend from school. In the dream, instead of my friend's voice, the crystal-clear voice of my father came on the other end. I had no doubt; it was definitely his voice. The voice said, 'Hello Paul.'

Astonished, I asked, 'Is that you, Dad?'

'Yes, it is,' he said.

'Dad, I didn't know you'd be there.'

He said: 'I'll always be there.'

The next moment I was awake, and I knew that my father had passed away. I also knew that he would 'always be there' – in other words, that he was in heaven. He had only drawn near to God – to church and to His Word – in his later years, so his eternal destiny had by no means been a foregone conclusion. The dream settled any doubts in my mind about his salvation.

I telephoned my Mum in Australia. As soon as she picked up the phone, before she even mentioned a word, I said, 'Hello Mum. I know ...' She then confirmed that my father had indeed died a few hours earlier – at precisely the same time that I had had my dream.

How gracious and loving is our God. Through the dream He let me hear my father's voice again, preparing me for his departure; He saved my mother from having to break the sad news; and He gave me not only peace in the moment, but assurance concerning my father's eternal destiny.

Paul M. Harvey served in Spain from 1992–2007, working alongside the Spanish evangelical church. He and his wife Rose were on the WEC leadership team from 1998.

A HAPPENING IN JAPAN

Richard Owens

Edna and I were returning from Japan in March 1998 and needed to sort out various things before we could leave the field. One of our contacts at that time was a student studying at the Teacher Training University at the back of our house. Her name was Junko* and she came to our house on her way home for English conversation lessons with Edna. They also did some Bible study together. Her home was in the next county, but to get there involved negotiating a pass, taking about fifteen minutes over hills. (*Name changed to protect identity.)

At that time, our daughter Mai was studying Art History at Essex University in Colchester, and one day she sent us the prospectus for her university. When we shared that with Junko about November 1997, she saw that there were courses for learning English there. She was due to finish her studies in March 1998 (the Japanese school year runs from April to

March), so could she return with us at the close of her studies in Japan? The six months until Essex opened in October would then give her a better acquaintance with English.

We had already booked our flight, so she arranged to fly the day after us and we met up in London. Once we had unpacked and were settled back in Anglesey, we wondered if there was a course in English Conversation for overseas students near us. Ah! There was one at Chester and we had a friend whose daughter was now living and teaching in Chester. Did she have a room? Sure enough, there was room for Junko and she would be able to go with her housemates to Borras Park Evangelical Church.

There were many new experiences for her at Chester, but she persevered. And eventually, she entered Essex University for their English course. We were able to keep in good contact with her and made occasional visits to Colchester. We met her parents when they came over for her graduation, but on her return to Japan, we were not able to re-connect with her. We did not know what had happened.

About six months later, we had the opportunity to make a return visit to Japan for the 50th Anniversary of the Ohtsu Church we had ministered at for ten years. Junko had taken us to her home to meet her parents on one occasion, but we didn't have the exact address. So, one day, we crossed the hills to her village and began going up and down various gorges that joined together at the village square. But we failed completely and had to return home. We could continue to pray for her.

We now jump forward ten years without any contact with Junko, and by now Edna had cancer. Edna had been in and out of hospital several times and was getting weaker. She was conscious that the end was near, but there were various ones she wanted to meet. We made several trips by car without ever thinking that those were some of the last she would make. That was when she confided to my daughter Edi, 'I wish I could have met Junko once again.'

It was Sunday lunch time on February 13th 2013 when Edna slipped quietly to Jesus while Edi and I were sitting beside her. For the last four days she had been as it were in a coma – just breathing strongly, for she had been in her High School marching band playing the sousaphone. After the Thanksgiving Service, Edi returned to Japan and I settled down to pick up the jobs that had been put on-hold for six months.

By the summer of 2013, I was busy gathering berries and garden produce. Once that was done, I began making plans to visit Edna's family in Eastern America. That had to be done before the ice and snows of November set in, and I was able to set off on October 15th for three weeks. Once that was done, I began wondering when would it be appropriate to visit Japan, and for how long? It was much easier to leave my house over Christmas, so I began planning to spend Christmas 2013 in Japan. I did the flight plans over the telephone, giving dates to go for four weeks. Just as I was e-mailing Edi in Japan to tell her what dates I was booking for a visit, a message came in from the travel agent. To my surprise, she told me I had booked to go to Japan for ten weeks (in Japan, the months have numbers rather than names, and I had confused the second month with the third month). This was late on a Saturday so I thought, 'I will just ask for an adjustment on the Monday morning.' When I explained my dilemma at church that Sunday morning, one or two said, 'Why don't you just go for the ten weeks?' And that is what I did.

As I prepared my itinerary for those ten weeks, I remembered one thing I had done two months previously in America. For my last full week, I had had no mid-week engagements, so should I make a 700-mile dash to family in another state, or not? The couple with whom I stayed were very happy for me to stay and join in with their weekday engagements. There were breakfasts with friends, lunches for senior citizens, and a fireman's dinner, but they were happy for me to tag along. I was beginning to see the difference between arriving at a place just for the Sunday morning, or being at a place to share in their week-day life as well. So now (for Japan) I asked my daughter to arrange visits to ten churches, but not just to go on the Sundays. Please could I come from the Wednesday evening of one week until the Wednesday morning of the next week? The weekday activities of each church were quite unique, but I was available to participate in the day-to-day life of the church and not just to be there for its Sunday morning service.

At this time, Edi and family had moved about thirty miles further south from where Edna and I had been located, to be close to an American High school (KIU) where their children could do Secondary School studies in English. KIU also held a bilingual English/Japanese worship service in their school hall, and Edi made the request, 'Daddy, you must keep one Sunday to be at KIU.' So, I kept my last Sunday to worship with them there.

So, here I was on my last Sunday morning of this trip to Japan, and Edi and I came to the meeting fairly early. Five or six rows of ten chairs each had been arranged in a semi-circle and a few worshippers had arrived. We made towards the front and spied three vacant seats next to a lady with two children. We sat next to them and after a while we exchanged greetings. Just then, as Edi and the lady looked at one another, she said, 'I am sure I know you.' The three of us could only gasp. I could do nothing but burst into tears at the Lord's kindness. So, how was it that Junko was there? The answer to that question was just as remarkable as my being there that Sunday morning.

One of the teachers at the KIU school was living with his family in a township about ten miles from the school, commuting each day to KIU. When he understood that there was an English man married to a Japanese lady in his area, he visited them and invited them to the bilingual worship service. The husband wasn't interested, but the lady would come every three or four months with her children, then aged five and nine.

There were so many things to share together once the service was over. All we could do was to confess that our Heavenly Father is well able to guide and to answer the heart cries of His children. Yes, the Lord had arranged for Edi and me to meet Junko on this one particular day! On Junko's New Year card for January 1st, 2019, she wrote that she had been baptised two months earlier.

Oh, what a privilege to know and be known by such a God!

Richard and Edna Owens served in church planting in the Kansai area of Japan, 1965–98.

27

GOD GAVE IT TO YOU

Liz Cleak

'God gave it to you … just take it and use it!'

These words from my Muslim neighbour Idris, a senior official at our bank in N'Djamena, capital of Chad, were just the encouragement we needed.

In 1989, I was acting as treasurer for our small but growing team as we faced a big project with no human prospect of the funds to accomplish it. Then, to our amazement, a large sum of money unexpectedly appeared in our bank account! I checked back to WEC home offices asking if they had sent the unexpected gift. No, they were not the source. Then I double-checked with other mission groups within Chad … negative responses again; no money was missing. Finally, I asked the bank to investigate the source of the transfer via their head offices in Paris. After a very long wait, they responded that they could no longer trace it, as the delay had been too great. It was definitely our money!

Chad had been through a period of devastating civil war during the late 1970s and 80s, which closed down our ministry in Abéché, the main town. Our small property was unoccupied for years, until the invading Libyan army took a fancy to it and bricked up the windows to slits, the better to shoot from. The mess they left behind was not improved when other soldiers thought the sheets of roofing iron would be useful for the decrepit airport buildings nearby. During the rainy season this resulted in the mudbrick inner walls crumbling … a final blow was a parting gift from the Libyans, when a bomb they dropped to destroy the airport went astray and caused the complete collapse of the bigger house. Surprisingly, the smaller, older house withstood the blast.

As a new government took over and life settled down, the local authorities began to put pressure on us to bring the wrecked property back into use. We managed to repair the older house and accommodate a family of new workers in it. But with their two small children, they were living alongside a building site. Another two families rented housing in town, but this was proving expensive … we really needed to get our property back into use, especially as other young families were preparing to join the team. Abéché was our centre for Arabic language learning.

So, praise God, we rebuilt that house with the mysterious funds. There have been many changes and developments since, but yes, God did indeed give us that money!

Liz Cleak served in Chad from 1976–2000, living among the unreached Barma people for about fifteen years; for part of that time, she was also co-leader of the Chad branch.

28

FLOUR FOR CONFERENCE

Margaret White

We really needed flour. Although we usually ate rice or cassava like our African neighbours, we liked bread for breakfast, especially during our annual missionary get-together. We would be hosting it for about fifty people, including our children, and everybody looked forward to bread as a wee treat. There was no bakery, but our house-helper baked beautiful bread and biscuits. We were nearly out of flour which we bought in 50 kg sacks in town fifty miles away.

It was time for our monthly shopping trip. It was hot and humid as our driver Rubeni skilfully manoeuvred our new Sherpa pick-up truck over the deeply rutted dry-season road, sending clouds of choking red dust billowing behind us. We parked under our usual shady tree near the market, where a group of small boys usually knew where to find the items we were looking for in return for a wee tip to buy their food for the day. Batteries, mantles for Aladdin lamps, pens, notebooks, duplicator ink and reams of paper. It was going well.

Then into the town centre for cases of margarine, corned beef and pilchards, cartons of matches, jerrycans of cooking oil, and sacks of rice, beans, sugar, and flour. It was going really well. Except that we couldn't find flour ... anywhere. There was no flour in town.

After a quick lunch with friends (who confirmed the town was out of flour) we started for home, a bit disappointed, but after all, bread isn't essential. On the outskirts of town, a policeman stopped us and asked for the Sherpa's MOT certificate. I explained that we didn't need one as the Sherpa was new. Maybe the heavy coating of red dust was hiding the shiny new paint. Or maybe he thought I'd bribe him to get on our way. He kept insisting we needed it and hopped on to direct us to his office.

The office was shut, and the 'man with the key' wasn't around either. The policeman insisted we drive him to their other office back in town to get the required certificate. Hot, sticky, tired and disappointed that we were going home without flour, I gave in with very poor grace and told Rubeni to just go where he said, so that we'd get home before dark. Of course, that office had no paper to do a certificate! I was ready to explode with frustration but stomped off to the shop next door to buy them some paper ... and saw a lorry stopped outside, piled high with sacks of flour! Ten minutes later, with our flour loaded and our MOT in hand, we were on our way home. That's the only time I was ever asked for an MOT.

Thank You, Lord, for keeping us in town 'til the flour arrived.

All things work together for good to those who love God and are called according to His purpose. (Rom. 8:28)

Margaret White served in Zaïre (now the Democratic Republic of Congo) from 1970–1996. On returning to the UK, she continued to serve God in her home-town of Coatbridge, near Glasgow. Now in her eighties, Margaret (like many other WEC retired members) has adapted smoothly to modern methods of communication, such as WhatsApp, Zoom etc.

STRATEGIC ENCOUNTER

Grace McNeill

It was early February 1999. My 95-year-old mother had just died, and we had her funeral a week later. Her memorial service was to be in Inverness where she had lived with my father for many years. I wasn't able to attend the memorial service, for by then I was on my way to Asia for several months to release one of my colleagues who was going home on sick leave. My journey involved three planes. First from the UK to Dubai, then Bangkok, then on to my destination. The first flight took off late in the evening.

I had a window seat in a row of three. Next to me was a lady, a member of a group of ladies travelling to India. On the other side of her was a gentleman who was on his way to Bangkok, on business. When he realised the lady sitting between us had friends in another row, he swapped with one so she would have company. It was quite a good flight, and as we were coming into Dubai the gentleman came back to his own seat to gather his belongings. And he started chatting. He began by telling us he'd never been to Bangkok but had lived and worked for some time in Africa.

Me: Whereabouts in Africa?

Him: The Ivory Coast.

Me: That's on the West of Africa, isn't it? In the bulging coast?

Him: Yes, how do you know that?

Me: Well, I travel, and I'm interested in Geography. What work did you do in the Ivory Coast?

Him: I was a teacher in an English-speaking school.

Me: Was it headed up by a lady called... Jean?

By this time there was a stunned/amazed look on his face.

Him: Yes, why ... how do you know that? Do you know her?

Me: Yes, I have known her for years!

Conversation finished at that point as we were disembarking from the plane, but as we were both going on to Bangkok we stayed together. It was almost midnight, but we found where to buy a coffee. It also gave us more time to talk.

I discovered that he had taught at Jean's school but had left abruptly over some difficulties and unresolved issues. He didn't say what. On returning to England, he had a family life, but no stable job; nothing seemed to be right! He was an unhappy man, and so discouraged. Being where we were in the airport, in the middle of the night, I was careful in what I said, and how I said it. But *something* had to be said:

> Me: You've never been happy since you left the school, have you?

> Him: No, I haven't.

> Me: I think that has to be sorted out, not just with the school, but with the Lord Himself. Don't you? (At this, he agreed with me). Once you've done that, you'll find His help in, and through, your problems.

He'd told me that he had some days in Bangkok for business deals, and a few days holiday in Thailand. So, I suggested he made time there to think and pray over what had caused him to leave the school, and the problems since then. He said he would. We went to the departure lounge for our next flight, and I found (having somehow not seen it before) in a pocket, a leaf from a Keswick Convention text calendar tab. Now our flights were in February – the paper had a July date! I looked at it and passed it over to my friend (I can't remember now what was on that paper, but I knew it was for him). He looked at it – 'It's meant for me!' he said. We parted at the gate, and I never saw him again.

At the '99 WEC Staff Conference, Jean Barnicoat was there. I caught up with her and asked her if this gentleman's name 'rang bells.' Did she know him? Of course she did!

Why did I ask? So I told her all about this meeting and conversation.

Jean, and her colleagues at the school, felt this man's departure keenly. It was a very difficult, depressing and distressing time at the school. It hurt, and they could not see past it – except knowing that God did. So they prayed and prayed. They didn't know how or where to find him. Where was he? *How* was he? All they could do was ask God to care for this man and bring him back to Jesus. And for Jean, the thrill of being assured God had not abandoned him!

I know no more than this. I wonder if he did take that extra time to sort himself out? What's happened to him since that encounter? I, for one, am truly convinced God rests only after the work is done. It's a long time since 1999, but I'm so glad God made me take that trip, even if it was just a couple of days after my mother's funeral.

Grace McNeill served with Radio Worldwide from 1965–72. During the years since, she has made numerous trips to Asia to help out with WEC conferences, for example, with the children's ministry.

30

ONLY ONE PERSON

Thelma Mills

'Could you please teach me to read in Balanta?'

A young man I didn't know, from a church near where I lived, earnestly asked the question. He could already read fluently in Portuguese, and also in Creole, the lingua franca used widely in Guinea-Bissau, where many different tribes lived, whose native languages were very varied. However, he wanted to find out how his heart language was written too.

That afternoon was the weekly meeting of our WEC missionaries living in, or visiting Bissau, so I happened to mention the lad's request. I was surprised when one or two of them felt that my schedule was too crowded to spend time with just one person. It was to be my final term in Guinea, and I was racing against time to complete the translation and writing up of the New Testament in that language, so they advised me to get on with the main task.

However, Yabna was persistent, and proved an apt pupil, picking up rapidly the alphabet as used in his language. Within a matter of weeks he had not only mastered the ability to read it, but had also written his testimony in the language and showed it to me.

At the time I was working on producing an oral version of Luke's Gospel, using the most fluent readers in Balanta to voice the spoken parts. Yabna was interested in this, and was given the part of Jesus, so becoming a frequent visitor to record his part. Eventually, one day, he shared that he felt God was burdening him to teach Balanta literacy, and share in the translation work, but he knew that he needed Bible School training first of all. He spent his practical year from our Bible School helping me with the Balanta translation for half his time, and the other half working with his church.

Today, he is the Youth Pastor of a large WEC-founded church of 1,000+ members, with several hundred young people to care for, with a wife and four children of his own, and heading up the Balanta literacy project. Yabna is also a Bible Society Consultant, overseeing the translation of the Old Testament into two other languages used in Guinea-Bissau – WEC missionaries, Isa Arthur and Lily Gaynor, having completed the New Testaments – plus two more languages with native speakers beginning translation of the New Testament. In addition, he is very involved in heading up the translation of the Old Testament into Balanta, the New Testament having finally arrived in Guinea in 2012.

With God, 'only' one person counts!

Thelma Mills served the Lord in Portuguese Guinea, later renamed Guinea-Bissau, West Africa, from 1962–2004, through medical and midwifery ministry, and also in translation of the New Testament into Balanta (one of many tribal languages).

END OF TERM PICK-UP

Amy Cuthbert

December 1983

I had left my passport in Bissau to have a visa stamped in for my trip to Senegal to bring the girls home for Christmas. One day, a lad arrived by canoe from Bissau (a ten-hour journey) with one document I had failed to sign! He returned with it the next day to Bissau.

From our home in Bubaque I travelled to Bissau by plane, to then travel on up to Senegal with Sue Goodman for us to collect the children for Christmas. Of course, we had to be there for the end-of-term Christmas production, which was always amazing. School finished on 23rd December, and we were booked on a plane to Bissau that afternoon. The plane would come from Dakar, stop in Ziguinchor near where the school was, and then on to Bissau. But the plane flew overhead without stopping! Obviously, it had filled up in Dakar. We had to return to the mission HQ in Ziguinchor.

What to do? Our colleague Bob Pritchard was soon on the phone to the airline in Dakar and had the promise that the plane would come again next morning at about 8:00 a.m. That evening, Bob and Sue put on a film evening for the kids and some games.

Next morning, 24th December, we were at the airport early – waiting. We waited – and waited – and waited. The kids were playing around. Judith was hopping about, 'I'm going to see my Daddy!' Jayne quietly played but I could see she was thinking the same – but sensing the apprehension of Sue and me as the hours passed. As I opened my mouth to say, 'It's not going to come,' we heard the roar of the plane and could see it in the distance. It was now about 11:00 a.m. We piled in, but I was thinking: 'How will we get to Bubaque for Christmas Day?' Norman, Robert and Susan were in Bubaque, as were all the Christmas presents that family had sent from Northern Ireland. Hazel was waiting for us in Bissau to come to Bubaque with us.

Tony Goodman met us in Bissau with the news that he had sent a message on ahead with the boat that we would not make it. The boat had left around midday and would take about six hours to get to Bubaque. Also, the last plane (a six-seater) had already left for Bubaque – there had been several that morning as it was Christmas Eve.

On a whim, I asked Tony to see if the pilot would do another trip. It did not occur to me that I was, in effect, asking to charter a plane! I didn't ask how much it would cost. I just knew that God would see that these excited children would be home to see their Daddy for Christmas. Tony found the pilot and he agreed to fly – if we could find the fuel! Tony rushed back to the Bissau HQ – got Hazel to grab her washing off the line (by now she thought she was going nowhere) – and came back with the fuel.

The pilot agreed to take us. We flew over the boat taking the message that we would not make it for Christmas! So, we were HOME FOR CHRISTMAS! God is so good.

We found out later that it cost 14 contos (worth about £100 at the time). There had just been a devaluation of the conto so it was half that price – and Hazel offered to pay half also. The school decided to close earlier for Christmas in subsequent years so that there was no panic for parents and children travelling.

Amy and Norman Cuthbert served in Guinea-Bissau 1975–1991. On returning home, they were WEC Co-ordinators for Ireland 1992–1999; UK Deputies & HQ Managers 1999–2007; Directors for all Ireland 2007–2016. They now live in Northern Ireland.

32

ANGEL UNAWARE?

Stan and Gwen Hawthorne

One evening of early winter in the mid 1970s, before the snow fell on the upper mountains in Kashmir, a man knocked at our door. Our children were in bed, and my wife and I were about to retire. I looked at my wife wondering who the caller could be at this time of night. People in the mountains usually go to bed early in winter when it gets dark and cold.

I went and opened the inner door, and the light shone on to a dark figure. He was serious in aspect, with a black beard and an awareness in his eyes. A fine figure of a man. He wore a black coat buttoned up to the neck and a wide brim black hat.

Before unlocking the outer screened door, I asked what I could do for him. He explained that he was a stranger in the area and had tried to get into the tourist bungalow up in the bazar, but it was full. They had informed him to go down to the house where the foreigners lived; they would put him up for the night.

I was silent for a moment staring at him, then for some unknown reason I opened the door and welcomed him in.

I introduced him to my wife, who then went into the kitchen to prepare him a meal. I begged him to sit down at the table. He sat down and took off his hat. He looked dignified and awesomely handsome. He could have stepped right out of the Old Testament. He didn't speak much until after he had eaten. Then he wished to sit on the floor, so we sat down with him.

All he wanted to talk about was God, Jesus and what we were doing in this village. He spoke simply and his words were so stimulating and enlightening.

It was getting late into the night and it was time to go to bed. I took a candle, lit it and escorted him along the outside verandah, down the stairs to the other end of the house to our guest room. It had the bare essentials – a bed, a table, a chair and of course the candle. The electricity in our village was always weak. I bade the guest goodnight and said I would see him again in the morning.

At seven o'clock the next morning I went down to call him but found the door slightly ajar. Looking inside the room I found he had gone. And the bed appeared not to have been slept in.

Stan and Gwen Hawthorne served in Asia from 1965–1991 and now reside in Northern Ireland.

SAFEKEEPING

Dave Northcote

I have held many things in my hands and lost them all, but whatever I place in God's hands, that I will always possess.
(Martin Luther)

As Mike Burden* stepped out of the door and began to descend the boarding ladder to the waiting bus below, a tsunami of thick, smelly, humid, boiling air flooded over him. The blast took his breath away and knocked the remainder of his energy from his body so that he dragged his feet along the alien tarmac to the vehicle, worn out with stress and fatigue ... (*Mike Burden is a pseudonym).

This is how one of my sons expressed his thoughts when they landed in yet another country to continue their education two-and-a-half days' journey from our place of ministry. It brought our sons' tally to six, not counting the two years we home-schooled them. Fortunately, God gave us a conviction that their childhood experiences were to be an integral part of our calling to this particular assignment.

Years before, we had taken them to a boarding school called Chefoo, situated in the Cameron Highlands, Malaysia. On the day that we were to part with them, they were too excited by all the new sounds and sights of this idyll in a tropical jungle to concern themselves with its implications. Standing in the doorway of the headmaster's house, they waved and smiled as we parted from view under our umbrellas that were attempting to shield us from the Monsoon rains. We wondered why we bothered trying to keep the rain out as we were getting soaked from the tears streaming down our cheeks. Our next news of them would come three weeks later in an aerogramme …

Some months later, we went to the local airport to meet their flight for the Christmas break. The outside temperature had plummeted to around −28°C and sure enough, there they were in T-shirts and shorts, grateful for all the extra layers we brought with us. As the taxi made its way back to our apartment, stories of their adventures tumbled out from the two lads. Seriously poisonous snakes were probably the biggest hazard, but there were plenty of other wild animals to instil in them a healthy respect for their 'adventure playground.' They never went off alone and someone in the group always carried a machete. When we were back in UK for furlough, these stories would reappear in the playground at the local school, but nobody believed them until one day the teacher asked the class for photos of activities they particularly enjoyed. How attitudes changed when the evidence arrived and suddenly everyone wanted to know more.

Their next school was a brand-new project in Northern Thailand called Grace International School (GIS). Getting the school officially registered took much longer than anticipated and, since our sons were in the initial intake, they were only issued with six-week tourist visas, which meant someone had to escort them out of the country every six weeks to get the visa renewed. On one occasion, we took the train south to Penang on the coast of Malaysia and stayed overnight at an American school in its exotic location right on the beach. The journey back was tortuously slow as the monsoon rains had all but concealed the track, but as I reflected on all the separation we faced, I was grateful for the extra experiences we could share together.

Despite these wonderful experiences, India was to test them at another level. Friendships and peer groups are all important in a child's development and none more so than when entering teenage years. Our eldest son's best friend in Cheefoo went to Hebron School in India for his secondary education so naturally my son wanted to go there too; but Thailand had seemed a more convenient option as links for travel between our ministry country and India were poor. However, travelling to Thailand to fulfil visa requirements on such a regular basis was not good, and by the time we reverted to using Hebron school his friend had returned to UK – so there was much disappointment at the start. We often talked about keeping friendships going in spite of separation and in a half-hearted way there was a resignation to a grain of truth I was sowing.

My wife and I had drawn much comfort during the absences from these words from Jeremiah 24:6 ... 'My eyes will watch over them for their good, and I will bring them back to this land. I will build them up and not tear them down; I will plant them and not uproot them.'

But even I could not have anticipated what was to follow years later when my eldest son returned to UK to begin his university education at Aberystwyth. On his first day after settling into his room, a student asked if he knew about the BBQ on the beach run by the Christian Union that evening.

He wandered down to the beach only to be greeted by two fellow Cheefoosians who happened to be starting their degree course there too. One of them was the very friend he was expecting to spend time with at Hebron school!

And finally ... by going to Hebron school my younger son married a classmate from the USA who had shared those school experiences, and the elder son grew to love India and settled there for his writing career and met his wife at church. Both were married the same year, filling my heart with the wonder of all the ways the Lord takes care of what is closest to one's heart when placed in His hands.

Dave and Becky Northcote served in the Far East 1993–2005. Dave was deputy branch leader for eight years before returning to the UK where he now has a role co-ordinating the care of many of the contributors of this publication. His first wife Becky having passed away, he is now married to Meg. They live in East Sussex.

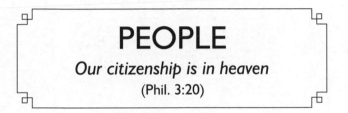

PEOPLE

Our citizenship is in heaven
(Phil. 3:20)

JUBILEE YEAR

Hazel Wallis

In 1990, the Evangelical Church of Guinea-Bissau decided to celebrate their 50th Anniversary by individual churches doing outreach to parts of the country without churches. So, we decided to challenge the church in the Bijagos islands to join in. I had seen how the cohort of young men who were about to go into the initiation rites the following year did a tour of all the thirty odd villages on the island of Uno, dancing and celebrating, accompanied by their wives and girlfriends; we suggested that we did something similar to celebrate the church anniversary.

The elders of the two churches on Uno supplied some rice and money and about ten of us set out, equipped with our grass mats, to go and preach the Gospel.

All went well for the first few days, when we introduced ourselves to the village committee. They showed us somewhere to sleep and summoned the whole village to a meeting where we could share. Then, about halfway round the island, we were in one village and had to cross the river to get to the next one. We had to leave then, because a troupe from another village about to go to the initiation rites were on their way to the village. We could hear their drumming, so at dusk we crossed the river which was deeper than we realised (or perhaps we missed the path across). As a result, everyone got thoroughly wet – one lady's six-week-old baby who was resting on her shoulder got his feet wet and for another one, tied to his mother's back, the water reached up to his nose.

Once we were over the river, we re-grouped and went on to the next village. They did not want to receive us and suggested we continued on to the next, slightly bigger, village. I think they didn't want to feed us, not realising that we had our own supper, bowls of rice and fish, with us. We later found out that they were also entertaining another initiation troupe. But the next village did receive us, and we were shown into two good rooms and could use the communal bathrooms. The next day the village committee arranged for us to share with the village in the early afternoon, which was not a good time as everyone was still in the fields. We knew we were in a spiritual battle! But we seized the opportunity and then went back to visit the village that had not wanted us the night before. On house-to-house visits, we were made welcome.

That evening after supper, the young people sat outside on the verandah and sang, which attracted all the local young people. Once there was a crowd, someone produced the visual aid, and the Gospel was preached. So, the Gospel was clearly preached in the village of Ancamona!

Hazel Wallis served from 1983–2009 in Guinea-Bissau, on the Bijagós Islands.

A NEW NAME

Paul M. Harvey

(Some details have been adapted to protect identity)

You will be called by a new name. (Isa. 62:2)

Soledad (pronounced Sollaydath) was one of the living pillars of the *Iglesia Evangélica* (Evangelical Church) in the Spanish town where we worked. She was faithful as the leader of the ladies' group, consistent at prayer meetings, wise with advice, and always ready to help people in need. She was a real Lydia or Dorcas from the Bible – an example to others, hard-working and loved by all. Her name Soledad is a shortened form of María de Soledad, meaning Mary of Solitude. We shall see the significance of solitude, or loneliness, in her story as it unfolds ...

Soledad had always been a religious person, a pious Catholic in a traditionally Catholic country. She recited her *Ave Marías* (Hail Marys), presented flowers to *La Virgen* (the local icon representation of the Virgin Mary), and followed the processions through the streets during *Semana Santa* (Holy Week), dressed in black when the occasion required. But she knew something was missing in her life.

When her eight-year-old daughter was invited to a children's club one summer, Soledad let her go. It turned out the club was run by evangelical missionaries, and the daughter was captivated by the stories about Jesus. It was because of her daughter and through these WEC missionaries, that Soledad herself discovered the Gospel message that we are saved by grace, though faith in Christ, rather than by following rituals and good works. From then onwards, she was a transformed person – 'born again' to use the words of Jesus in the Bible.

It would help at this point to explain the background to name-giving in Spain during the days of the dictator General Franco. From the time Franco gained power after the Spanish Civil War (1936–39) until his death in 1975, his regime kept a tight lid on Spanish society – and this included providing a definitive list of names from which parents had to choose when christening their babies. By law, names had to be religious or traditional, according to the list – hence the popularity of double-barrelled names containing Joseph or Mary, such as José-María, José-Luís, José-Manuel (boys) and María-José, Mari-Carmen, Mari-Angeles (girls). Particular Catholic doctrines or themes would also appear in name-form – Dolores (the pains/sufferings of Christ), Concepción (the immaculate conception of the Virgin Mary) and so on. The name María de Soledad was also on the list.

The years after the Civil War were harsh and poverty-stricken, with many families having been torn apart by ideological differences. In the years that followed, Soledad was given away as a child by her mother to be brought up by another woman. Her own family became a vague memory and the name she had been given, 'Loneliness,' in a real sense had come true. As far as blood relatives were concerned, she was alone in the world.

And so it was, years later when we knew her as a shining example of Christian faith, that a remarkable event occurred. Soledad shared with the church fellowship that she had been contacted by the national television programme 'Hay Una Carta Para Ti' (There's A Letter For You). This was a prime-time, reality-style programme in which separated relatives were brought together 'on air' after years, sometimes decades, apart. The invitation had come for her to appear live on the programme to discover 'the secret' of who was trying to make contact with her. Soledad was suspicious of the whole thing, believing it could be a prank to embarrass or even deceive her. She'd decided to ignore it – but there remained the gnawing possibility in the back of her mind that it could be genuine. She asked for prayer, and we all asked God for wisdom and guidance.

At last, she came to the decision to attend the programme; so when the night arrived, we were all glued to our televisions. The finale to the show approached and on to the stage came our sister-in-Christ, Soledad, to be duly quizzed by the show's presenter. Behind a screen, unseen to Soledad, was a man whom the audience had previously been told was her long-lost brother. But how would Soledad react? Would she remember him? Would she be pleased, or distraught? The orchestra played, the tension mounted, all in the manner loved by such reality viewing. The studio audience, as well as the millions watching on TV, held their breath.

At last the screen was removed, and the man was presented to his sister Soledad. For several seconds she stood there in total shock, until the truth dawned on her – then she burst into tears. So did the brother, so did the presenter, so did we and most of the audience too. The show, a resounding hit, ended with the protagonists smiling and embracing. After a lifetime, Soledad had been reunited with her brother!

Once back in the church fellowship, Soledad told us how she had seen the Lord's hand at work throughout the experience. It was all genuine: the man was indeed her brother, and she was now reunited with her wider, long-lost family. She told us: 'The programme was the means, but it was God who gave me back my family.' To express her joy, she decided to take on a new name, Lydia, chosen directly from God's Word rather than from Franco's prescribed list.

She was no longer Mary of Solitude – Loneliness – because she now truly belonged to her own natural family, as well as to the family of God.

Paul M. Harvey served in Spain from 1992–2007, working alongside the Spanish evangelical church. He and his wife Rose were on the WEC leadership team from 1998.

36

CULTURE SHOCK

Jean Goodenough

One of the problems a missionary candidate is warned to expect is culture shock. This occurs when two different cultures come into contact. In England, it can happen when someone who takes milk straight out of the bottle meets someone who always pours it into a jug first. When going abroad, the differences, and therefore the shock, are greater.

I am glad God did not call me to a country where it is polite to show one's appreciation of a meal by burping loudly. Although I am able to burp, I cannot do it to order. One time I mentioned this to a youth group, making the comment that if a person were gifted in this respect maybe God was calling him to be a missionary in a country where it is acceptable. As soon as I said this, the whole group turned round and looked at one boy sitting at the back!

Incidentally, reverse culture shock can also take place. Imagine the poor missionary who has adapted to expressing their appreciation in this way. When they come home, they have to break the habit pretty quickly if they are to be socially acceptable.

My own culture shock in the Ivory Coast came as a result of having to greet people. In England we usually only shake hands with strangers or on formal occasions, such as leaving church. But in many countries, you are expected to shake hands with the people you see every day. This took some adjusting to, but I tried hard, until I felt I was shaking hands all the time.

So, it was quite devastating when Wolfgang told me I was not greeting people properly. 'I don't understand,' I said, 'I'm shaking hands all the time.'

'No,' replied Wolfgang. 'Sometimes you come over to our house while I am talking to someone and you don't greet the person.'

The penny dropped. In our culture, if we call on someone and find they already have visitors, our reaction is to back away as quickly as possible, unless we are specifically invited to come in. It is rude to interrupt and we fear it. By contrast, in Africa it is quite permissible to interrupt and it would be rude *not* to greet everyone. Now I found the two cultures in direct conflict. In the end, I compromised. If I wanted to see the Kriegs, I would go over to their house and try to determine from a distance if they had visitors. If they did, I would slink away unnoticed, thereby satisfying my own instincts not to interrupt and at the same time avoiding giving offence to others. What the eye doesn't see the heart doesn't grieve over!

After I had been in the country for a couple of months, a missionary with another society asked me how I was settling in. I replied that I liked it and was not suffering too much from culture shock. He then warned me of 'secondary culture shock' which may occur more than six months later. At this point the initial fascination with the country has worn off, and the new missionary is exposed to the problems her senior colleagues face every day.

It wasn't until my second term of service that I really came up against a chronic problem for many missionaries. Basically, it is 'white equals rich.' People were always asking me to lend them money. It seemed that being in debt was an accepted part of African culture, whereas the Scripture tells us to 'owe no man anything' (Rom. 13:8). It also says, 'When someone wants to borrow something, lend it to him' (Matt. 5:42). I began to get tied up in knots over the whole business.

As I thought and prayed about it, I saw a practical solution to the borrowing question. Each month I put aside a 'second tithe.' This was earmarked for lending to people in need. That solved the command in Matthew chapter 5. At the same time, I stressed to the borrower that I could only lend money once. Under no circumstance could I lend money a second time if the first debt was unpaid. Hopefully, this would encourage the Christian to heed the instruction in Romans to 'owe no man anything.'

Jean served in the Ivory Coast (Côte d'Ivoire) from 1976–1983 and thereafter at the UK headquarters in various roles. She says: 'If my mother had not gone on to the streets to invite strangers to Church, she would never have met my father; so anything I have done is a consequence of my mother's desire to bring others to Jesus.'

37

REAL OR UNREAL?

Heather Donnelly

I worked in Senegal 1969–1978 and served amongst the Jola tribe, who mainly live in the south of the country, the Casamance. I was then Heather Grove (my maiden name) but the Jola's called me 'Mademoiselle Hedda' as they couldn't pronounce 'th' and had a whistle corresponding to my name which they used to call me.

I helped in a small clinic with another missionary (Iris Kinchin and later Mena Gilpin) in my village, but I mainly worked amongst the school children, teachers and the youth. I also distributed Bible Stories written in simple French by one of our missionaries, Sheila Kilkenny, and illustrated by Pamela Riches. I took these leaflets to about fifteen different village schools on my moped which often caught in the sand and I fell off, amusing many of the Jolas.

One day, going to one of the schools where the teacher was the older brother of a Christian (Marcel) in our small local church, I arrived to distribute the leaflets to his class. That day it was quite cold, and I had worn my tights. After greeting the teacher (Monsieur Orpah) I said, 'How cold it is today!' and pulled out a bit of my tight on one leg to show him what I was wearing. Immediately, the front row pupils ducked down below their desks in fear. They had seen, what they thought was my skin being pulled out away from my leg! Eventually one of the pupils, a boy, saw I had something covering my toes (my tights) and so sat up again and the rest of the row followed his example.

The next time I saw that teacher, he told me that as the children walked home after school, down the bush paths home, they kept looking for Mademoiselle Hedda's skin on the ground as they thought she may have shed her skin just like a snake! They also had tried to pull out the skin on their legs just like I had done to my tights.

Well, it reminds us that not everything is what we think it is – but we can always be sure of God's love and care for us.

Heather Donnelly served in Senegal, 1969–78, in a variety of roles including medical work, teaching in the agricultural Bible school and in youth/children's work. Thereafter, she served at the UK WEC headquarters. She now lives near Bristol.

38

EGGS OF GRATITUDE
Liz Cleak

'Cheep-cheep, cheep-cheep!'

Barbara and I were doing the washing up, not feeling very lively after the previous day's long trip on Chad's bumpy back roads. Puzzled, we looked around, and realised the noise was coming from the top of our kerosene fridge.

The day before, while waiting for the Pastor to finish his meeting with a group of Christians in a small village, I had gone to visit a woman who was poorly with a fever. I had brought some paracetamol and anti-malarial pills with me, so since there seemed no other reason for her sickness, I left a treatment with her, praying for her and explaining the dosage. As we left to drive home, her husband ran up and thrust a small package into my hands. It contained a few eggs which he insisted we must take home with us. In his gratitude for his wife's treatment, he was giving us the only thing he had to offer, these eggs which he had grabbed from under his broody hen!

Those eggs, already warm, had a long hot journey with us back to our village home. By that time, we had no further thought for the eggs and parked the little package on the top of the fridge, where the warmth ... yes, you've guessed it ... completed mother hen's job and out came a chick! Poor little motherless thing, he spent his early days in a box to keep him safe from our two cats. He grew up very brazen and constantly stole their food, so soon he found himself living outside with our other livestock. Then he had to be rescued from other chickens who did not accept him, until he grew to be a strutting cock determined to fight with all comers. We did not want to consign him to the pot, so we gave him to a friend who had only hens.

Throughout those years of village living, we frequently found ourselves receiving meals, peanuts, fish, pigeons and many other tokens of friendship. But 'Chuck' was the most memorable!

Liz Cleak served in Chad from 1976–2000, living among the unreached Barma people for about fifteen years. She now lives in Herefordshire.

39

INCONVENIENCES

Jean Goodenough

In the town of Oumé in the Ivory Coast we had electricity, most of the time, and running water, most of the time. Our house also had an inside flush toilet. Yet we spent a considerable part of our time in the villages. In the villages, there was no running water, no electricity and no inside flush toilet. Come to that, often there was no outside toilet either. At first, I found these three inconveniences very hard. It was oppressive at night when the only light came from dim oil lamps, the lack of water on tap was annoying, and as for the lack of loos ...

However, gradually I accepted the lack of electricity and running water. But the other matter bothered me throughout the whole of my first term. Only towards the end did I share with my senior colleague, Olive, how I felt about the inconveniences. I had assumed she was perfectly adjusted after twenty years on the field. But now came the shock; she *still* disliked the lack of toilet facilities!

What is more, she demonstrated it on our last visit to the villages. Going off to 'see George' as she put it, she returned more quickly than expected. Her only comment was, 'Too many people around!'

Going to the bush is the normal way of coping when there are no toilets. It has its hazards. A friend of mine visited the bush toilet in the dim light of dawn. A short distance away she glimpsed what she thought was an animal in the bush. Imagine her consternation when the 'animal' suddenly stood up and walked away on two legs.

Once I visited the bush after dark. I took my torch with me and turned it off, for obvious reasons, when I thought I had found a suitable spot. Suddenly I felt something crawling over my foot, then another something, lots of somethings. Grabbing my torch and dancing out of my sandals I saw that my 'suitable spot' was an ants' nest.

So, what do you do when the call of nature comes at night? The missionary is RFA – Ready For Anything. We have what we call a night tin. This is just an old tin, perhaps a coffee tin, which is a vital part of the missionary's equipment when on trek. If nature calls your host at night, he will simply pop outside his house. The missionary, however, will use the night tin and throw the contents out of the window. One night when a missionary threw the contents of her tin out of the window, she heard a bigger splash than she expected. She remembered with horror that, because it was the rainy season, the women had put their bowls under the eaves to catch the rain. Now one bowl had something extra. There was no alternative but to go outside and empty that bowl. It did not rain any more that night. Next morning it was like Goldilocks and the Three Bears when one of the women discovered her empty bowl and wanted to know why. My friend did not enlighten her.

Living in a developing country is exciting. When I returned for my second term, I was delighted to see that more villagers appreciated the luxury of a nearby outside toilet. 'Wee houses' were springing up in the villages like the television aerials in town. Maybe cockroaches do come out at night, but it is a vast improvement on ants' nests!

Jean served in the Ivory Coast (Côte d'Ivoire) from 1976–1983. She keeps active in ministry, as well as with swimming and table-tennis.

BOBO SHOPPING

Jo Parnell

How many carols and Christmas songs can you sing on a 180-kilometre road trip? Sue and I sang all the ones we knew as we returned home from the 'Bobo Shopping' trip one December day, sometime in the late 1970s.

Every month a couple from our missionary team, or two single ladies, took it in turns to spend a week in Bobo Dioulasso in Burkina Faso, shopping for the rest of the team. Living in the bush area of that inland African country, it was a real treat to go to 'civilisation ...' staying in a motel from another mission organization with running water (non-drinkable), electric lights and reliable fridges ... and flush toilets!

But it was no holiday as, armed with sometimes ten lists, we tackled the various requests. Several visits were made to the one supermarket in town (the size of a Tesco Express), hoping that butter and cheese had arrived by air from France. What did our folk from the USA mean by 'cream' (evaporated milk) and 'jelly' (jam)? This had caused confusion, so all lists had to be written in French.

Then on to local stores run by Burkinabes for cartons of 'Dutch Baby' dried milk, medical supplies for our clinic, visiting various offices for official paperwork, meat from the butcher (fewer flies there than in our local market!), car parts and of course, drawing the mission money from the Bank. Building supplies were sometimes required – bags of cement, metres of iron rods, plywood panels as well as bottles of gas for our ovens. All needed to be collected and loaded on to the lorry of a local haulage truck to be delivered (hopefully) before we arrived back home.

In this busyness, it was so good to have fresh French baguettes and croissants every day. Also, it was a treat to visit a local restaurant run by Catholic nuns where the food was 'safe' to eat. Sitting outside under the stars on a warm evening, with the anti-mosquito coils slowly giving off protective smoke, made such visits very special. The final task at the end of the week was to go to the market or roadsides to buy fruit and vegetables for everyone.

So here we were on our way homeward bound. The 3CV Citröen Camionette was loaded with everything labelled, lists and money were finally sorted – how many times did we count the remaining money?! – cash we had drawn from the bank was hidden in a drum under kilos of potatoes, cool boxes filled and money for our stay paid.

Time was passing and it was getting very hot. The first road for about twenty kilometres out of town was tarmac, but then we hit the unmade 160-kilometre stretch. 'Washboard' describes the surface well and the Citröen bounced along on top of it. Holding the car on the road and not skidding was a tiring feat. Chickens scattered and dogs chased us as we passed through roadside villages. Then, after a lot of kilometres and a few carols, a warning light told of trouble with the petrol. No Automobile Association there … lifting the bonnet revealed no problem … but, looking under the car, we found that the pipe connecting the petrol tank to the engine had somehow become detached. How we fixed it I don't remember, but I know it was an answer to prayer. So off we went again … bobbing along and singing 'dashing through the snow.'

Jo Parnell worked in Burkina Faso, West Africa from 1970–1992 in a teaching and training capacity in literacy, children's work and supporting pastors and their wives. Since returning to the UK, her missionary heart has been evidenced in the numerous groups of children and teenagers she has personally taken to WEC camps, travelling with them to the venues, camping in the field and participating in activities – even into her eighties!

HOME FOR CHRISTMAS

Mary Pritchard

My tears dripped into the chicken! I was living in South Asia. I had never spent a Christmas lunch like this before. Feeling sorry for two friends who had returned home from a thirty-hour train journey the night before, I had invited them for lunch. But they had gone off to renew their visas. At least they could have let me know that they couldn't come! I thought of my family back home in the UK – all together and devouring the turkey.

The doorbell rang. At the door was one of the absent friends. He apologised that he and his wife had come back with a bad tummy bug. They had been trying unsuccessfully to phone a neighbour's phone all morning to tell me they couldn't make it.

I had thought it strange when they'd never appeared at the Christmas morning service. On the sub-continent it is a wonderful time, worshipping the Lord Jesus who, after all, is what Christmas is about. Somehow, time doesn't matter and without the tinsel and in the Eastern setting, it is more real. This is followed by 'Wishing.' You meet up with all your friends wishing them a good Christmas and spend as much time at that as you want. It had been a lovely morning.

But now, my friends needed Christmas in bed. So, I decided I would swap the chicken for 'humble pie.' I called at the home of a family who had invited me for Christmas explaining what had happened and asking if I could join them after all. With typical Asian hospitality my friends said, 'Oh just come in; we had been bored stiff, as no-one else has come yet!' The friends soon did come and their small flat was full of people.

We decided then that Christmas alone would never happen again. We often did eat together as a fellowship of believers in each other's homes. My niece, on receiving my letters in the UK, would say, 'Oh, she is at another party!'

Asian hospitality has to be 'felt to be telt.' Each Christmas Day that would be what would happen, after worship and 'wishing' was over. We chose one of the largest flats we had. Usually it was mine! It was an occasion to invite Muslim neighbours and friends who did not know the miracle of Christmas. Then everyone would cook really international fare. One Asian lady said she would get a pricey turkey for the two English ladies. We told her we preferred chicken! She said, 'Thank goodness, because if he had sold me a big old crow, I wouldn't know the difference.' Even other friends and neighbours would enjoy sharing our Christmas fare and fun. Once a lady went missing during the afternoon. I found her in my bed! She, being the mother of a large family, insisted it was the best Christmas she had ever had!

Another Christmas, I had just said 'Goodbye,' to the last guest. My Muslim neighbour from the flat above was at my door. 'Mary,' she said, 'this is your special day and I want to share it with you.'

So, the mince pies, etc., were shared out again! And we both sat there talking for a very long time.

Mary Pritchard volunteered with the WEC ministry SOON (evangelistic broadsheets) 1965–75, then with Neighbours Worldwide (Ministry among unreached people groups within the UK, 1975–82) before serving in Southeast Asia from 1984–96. On her return to the UK, she pioneered WEC's short term TREK ministry, and served again with Neighbours Worldwide in the Midlands until retirement in 2007.

CHRISTMAS IN BURKINA FASO

Jo Parnell

The sun has set. It is now cooler as we make our way under the amazing African night sky to join our Lobi brothers and sisters for our Christmas meal. Torches and lanterns, bobbing along, lead to a cleared area near the church. In the centre, large pots of cooked food await us. These are encircled by chattering children seated on the dusty ground, eyes bright and shining through the dark, empty bowls in front of them, excitedly anticipating the coming meal. We join the adults sitting behind them. Dogs who have followed their owners, growl and scuffle in the darkness.

For weeks, small money contributions have been collected for this meal which today will give a treat of rice (instead of usual daily millet porridge) and a few pieces of meat and peanut butter gravy.

Once most of the Christians and their families are seated, clapping starts and, accompanied by drums, songs of praises are joyfully sung. During this singing everyone's bowl is filled with rice and topped with the meat (including a few innards!) and gravy. Once all are served, our pastor gives thanks to God for His wonderful and indescribable gift of His Son and for the meal and fellowship we will enjoy. Then silence descends as eager fingers dip into the bowls and the simple but so appreciated meal is eaten.

Afterwards we chat, babies and younger children fall asleep, then more songs are sung until (several hours after we left home) we wend our way there again. Celebrations, begun in church in the morning, then this simple meal ends the special day of Christmas celebrations in the bush areas of Burkina Faso.

(I have written this in the present tense as not only was it celebrated like this when I was there, but it will still be celebrated, I am sure, in the same way, in the many churches out there this year, and every year).

COMING AND GOING

Amy Cuthbert

We arrived back in Bubaque, Guinea-Bissau, after a trip home to Northern Ireland, on 15th August 1985. I started home school with Robert and Susan but then had to interrupt this to take Jayne and Judith to BCS (Bourofaye Christian School). Mid-September we took them and had a week there settling them in and doing shopping. Just before going to Senegal, however, we had visited Lendem for a day. On the way to Lendem the vehicle hit a tree stump at the side of the road — we were going slowly on a rough road — and I jarred my neck. It seemed okay though I had a tingling feeling the rest of the day. We went to Bula to visit a friend and the discomfort increased. While in Senegal, I began to feel nauseous. Then I began to have a headache and the side of my neck began to swell.

8th October Bissau: While in Bissau waiting for a boat, we went to Cantchungo (the Chinese there had an X-ray machine) to have an X-ray on my neck. But the machine had broken down, so we went on to a doctor in Bissau – he was with the Swedish Embassy and arranged an X-ray in Bissau hospital. However, it was of such poor quality nothing could be confirmed. The doctor said I had torn a muscle and a large blood clot was developing which could become infected. Also, because of the severity of the damage, I might also have broken some small bones – any swift movement could dislodge one of these with grave consequences! He recommended I go home for investigation and treatment.

What to do? We had only just returned; I had started home school with Robert and Susan, and we had just left Jayne and Judith in school in Senegal. By now I was wearing a surgical collar and was feeling quite ill. A container which we had filled in Northern Ireland was due to arrive shortly and Norman would need to receive that and sort it out. So it was decided I should go home on my own. Friends would help Norman get the container to Bubaque and look after Robert and Susan on the boat journey. Hazel would then do school with them till I got back. And Eugenia (our house help) would be able to come to cook and clean (Eugenia later went to Bible College and married a Pastor. They then headed up the Youth for Christ centre in Bissau).

Previously, while on furlough in Northern Ireland, God had really spoken to me from Psalm 121, especially, 'The Lord will look after your coming and going.' What did that mean now? Church elders came and prayed for me, but I did not improve. On the morning I left we read and prayed, though I could hardly concentrate thinking of the distance I was putting between me and my little family. The reading was from Luke 6:46-49: 'The wise man built his house on the rock – and WHEN the storms came the house stood firm.'

Soon I was away. A heavy suitcase was out of the question as I could not carry it. I had a small, practically empty case. I flew to Dakar and had a day in the HQ there awaiting the flight to England. I spent the time lying flat in bed. I was so afraid to turn my head in case any of these bones became lethal! Anyway, I arrived in Heathrow, London, and realised I had to change terminals. It was the height of the 'Troubles' and anyone from Northern Ireland was suspect. None of the airport staff would help me – except one. I heard a strong Belfast accent saying, 'Come on love; I can't see a fellow-countryman in trouble.' He led me all the way through the terminals to Terminal 1. In Belfast, I could not lift my small case off the carousel and, despite the surgical collar I was wearing, no-one would help me. Of course, it could have contained a bomb! But my brother, Tom, arrived and all was well.

We talked and laughed all the way home. That evening, several family members called and again we talked and laughed. My predicament was hardly mentioned. It was just the release of tension I needed. The Minister from church called too. The next morning, I went to A&E and it was confirmed that I had an infected haematoma in my neck, but no bones were broken. Suddenly, I had a huge swelling on the side of my neck, and this was considered good as the infection was not spreading inwards. The surgeon had been a missionary in Brazil so spoke Portuguese. The next day I was operated on to drain it. This had to be dressed every few days after I was discharged from hospital. On the first occasion a student nurse was asked to hold my hand and talk with me throughout the procedure. Suddenly, I realised that I was holding her! She had been observing the procedure and fainted right out!

I had six weeks at home with my parents and younger sister. They re-arranged their home so that I could have a room to myself. I made a slow recovery and still needed a surgical collar when I left at the end of November. Friends and family were all very good and I had a big suitcase plus my little one when I left. Meta Dunlop's friends too wanted to send her some Christmas gifts. I had no problem getting them on the flight in Belfast – no extra baggage costs. Marie Harper, from the UK headquarters, Bulstrode, came to Heathrow to greet me and help me through the airport. When I went to check in, excess baggage was going to cost £140! Chocolates and Christmas cake weigh quite a lot, but I decided they were not worth £140. I sorted through the cases and got things down to about £47, which I considered reasonable. Marie was pleased with all that I off-loaded on to her. She could use them as Christmas presents for friends, so this was quite literally a 'God-send' for her! And I had enough left for us and Meta.

Folk from WEC helped me in Dakar and then I made the short flight to Bissau. It was great to be back with Norman and the family. By 1st December we were back in Bubaque. Then, by mid-December, Jayne and Judith were home for Christmas. I continued with the collar for several months and needed to rest. Hazel had kept up school with Robert and Susan and, in January, a short-term helper was due to come for six months to teach them.

With the help of family, friends and even strangers, the Lord had indeed 'looked after my coming and going.'

Amy and Norman Cuthbert served in Guinea-Bissau 1975–1991. They now live in Northern Ireland.

44

THE BEAUTIFUL BACHELOR

Betty Singleton

Young Dakori's eyes were not good, and the teacher would not let him attend the little school. So, he went at night and listened to the others, and thereby learned English. Eric Christie, missionary to Ghana, gave him the Scripture Gospel Mission booklet 'Way of Salvation.' He learned all the Scripture verses off by heart. He was sent by day to watch his mother's cows (sitting on the back of one of them) to make sure they didn't destroy anyone's vegetable garden – or so they called the bare ground which they hoed and planted.

His mother had taken him to the local fetish priest, offering the blood of a chicken mixed with cow dung, and putting it on Dakori's eyes, saying this would make his eyes better. But it didn't.

Dakori listened to the story of Jesus dying on the cross. One night he was tossing on his mat on the mud floor of his room with his body aching with fever. His Vagla people followed the 'way of the fetish.' That was the only way Dakori had known, but that night he cried to God and said: 'If Jesus is the true one and died for my sins, please help me. And Jesus, come into my heart.' God heard his cry, and he was saved.

He was the best drummer in their village of Soma. But village dancing at night was not always a good thing. Dakori decided to give it up. The village people called to him, 'Come and play the drums Dakori, come and play and sing.' But he answered, 'No, I will not come. I have given my life to Jesus. I will live for Him now.'

When we came to know Dakori, we took him to the eye specialist in Tamale but it was too late. The onchocerciasis had done its worst. The consultant told us: 'I'm sorry, we can't help this young man.' I wanted to cry, but Dakori said: 'Ma, don't cry. Even if I go completely blind, I will trust in Christ.' He has been true to his word, always witnessing for Jesus his Saviour.

The village women in Tuna said that no one would ever marry a blind man. How could he dig the ground to grow food? While he was a special student at the School for the Blind in Wa, some of the girls there said they would marry him. He asked them, 'Are you a Christian?' and if they said, 'No,' he said, 'Sorry, no way!'

The Torch Trust for the Blind invited him to their Annual Meeting in the UK and gave him two piano accordions to take home to Ghana for Norman and me. One Easter, he brought home a John's Gospel in Braille in English. He sat in the village and read it out aloud. The village people came excitedly to us and said, 'Dakori with no eyes is reading with his fingers and is giving us the Good News of Jesus!'

When he became a Church pastor, Dakori Viela of the Vagla tribe helped my husband Norman and me with translation. We also knew he had previously been the village drummer and had great natural musical ability. Both of us had a piano accordion, so I spoke to Norman and he agreed to give his accordion to Dakori. After getting the heavy Hohner strapped to his shoulders, I showed him where the 'key with the hole in it' was, and the place for the chords. After some noisy attempts, his musical talent found a way, and he soon got the hang of it. He composed his own Vagla Scripture songs and God blessed him to become an expert, bringing blessing to many through playing and singing to the glory of God. The Roman Catholic priest called by and said, 'That Evangelist of yours is a fine fellow. I wish I had one like that!'

I wrote to the British and Foreign Bible Society and a lady sent her deceased husband's thirty copies of the Braille Bible for Dakori. It took several mail bags to get them to us on the weekly mail bus. The first thing Dakori did was take the copy of Isaiah. Isaiah is very long, and came in two copies, so he said, 'Oh, this is the second book of Isaiah!' He found the verse of Scripture he had learnt from the SGM 'Way of Salvation' booklet years before.

You will remember that the women had said Dakori would never marry. Well, Afua came from the Dagaati tribe in Sutiopor. Her grandmother accepted Jesus when Norman and his colleague Dapla were preaching. We went one day to burn her fetishes, which she did not want any more now that she was a Christian. There was an animal skull and other bones and rubbish, plus a little bell she said she had called the spirits with. I took a bottle of paraffin to pour over the whole lot so it was well burnt up. Dapla sang, 'We are not afraid of Satan, Jesus is my Saviour!'

Afua helped her grandmother walk the three-and-a-half miles to Tuna for Church every Sunday morning, walking in front of her holding her stick. A passing car or lorry was very rare. Everyone walked on the road. Afua became a Christian too, and once she had grown up, Dakori Viela found a good girl who was more than willing to marry him! At their wedding, towards the end of the ceremony, Dakori's mother stepped forward and announced in a loud voice: 'Now I know that God can do anything! My Dakori Viela (which means "beautiful bachelor") has found a wife!' Dakori and Afua had seven children.

Norman and Betty (who is Australian) Singleton served in Ghana, 1953–1977. Their children, John and Anne, attended The Elms school, 1967–77. On returning to the UK, Norman and Betty headed up WEC's south regional office from Southampton, 1978–1983.

EARLY DAYS IN SPAIN

Paul and Rose Harvey

Part One

1992 was Spain's 'annus mirabilis' – its year of wonder. The Olympic Games took place in Barcelona, Madrid was Europe's Capital of Culture and Seville hosted Expo '92. Once those were all over, the Harvey family arrived in October, having been called to serve God in this predominantly Catholic, yet increasingly secular land.

A small flat on the fourth floor of an apartment block had been found for us, so with our two small children, plus belongings from home, we began to settle in. The flat was an empty shell. No beds, no furniture, no kitchen cupboards – nothing, apart from the toilet, bath and bidet in the bathroom, and a functional sink in the kitchen. No light bulbs anywhere, just a couple of wires hanging down through an untidy hole in the ceiling of each room.

It was a challenge to make the place habitable, partly through of our lack of DIY experience, but mostly through our lack of the language. Fifty metres down the road was a *ferretería* – not a 'ferret shop,' like it sounds, but an ironmonger (*ferrum* being the Latin for iron). This was an Aladdin's Cave, stocking everything for every project imaginable, but it had one drawback; you cannot just go in, buy something quietly off the shelf, pay anonymously and slip out. No, first you have to find out when it's your turn by announcing in a loud voice, 'Quién da la vez?' (Who gives the turn? i.e. who's the last person waiting?); then you have to ask the shopkeeper for your items while everyone listens in; then you respond to the shopkeeper's questions about size, quantity, colour and so forth. All in Spanish. After just a few days in the country, it's a big leap to move from 'Buenos días, me llamo Pablo' (Hello my name's Paul) to 'Hi there, I need a dozen light fittings, two metres of electrical cable, some wire cutters and a cross-headed screwdriver, you know, the Phillips type, and a box of half-inch, sorry I mean 1.5cm screws please – oh, with rawl plugs to match.' All in front of the waiting masses. I'd looked up 'rawl plugs' in the dictionary and found 'tacos,' but in the heat of the moment I mispronounced it 'tocas,' which translates as 'touches' or 'you touch.' Titters from behind do not bolster one's confidence.

Two weeks into our Spanish adventure, the flat was still in chaos and unpacked boxes still festooned the living room.

We had managed to install some light bulbs, hang some kitchen cupboards and assemble the beds for all four of us, but more jobs needed doing. I found myself back in the *ferretería* practising my Spanish in front of the crowd, when I noticed a large rectangular pinboard at the back of the shop. I immediately thought it would be ideal in the living room with photos on it to remind us of home, but I had no idea what the Spanish for 'pinboard' was. Never mind – it was within plain sight and a mere gesture along with a *'por favor'* (please) proved sufficient to convey my desire to buy it. I paid and left the shop, pinboard under my arm.

Next, I paid a quick visit to the *farmácia* (pharmacist), then the *estanco tobacos* (tobacco shop where they sell stamps) and finally *Ahorramas* (the *Save More* supermarket) for a few provisions. Half an hour later I was climbing the steps (no lift) to the fourth floor, shopping bags in hand, when I stopped. 'Have I forgotten something?' I thought. Light bulbs, paracetamol, stamps, milk, bread, bananas. That's all I went for. Wait a minute…the large, rectangular pinboard was missing from under my arm!

I left the shopping bags outside the door to our flat and rushed straight back to the supermarket, my last port of call. I recognised the cashier girl who had served me, and when she had finished with a customer, I tried to ask her if she had seen my pinboard. The problem was I had no Spanish for 'pinboard,' 'cork,' or even 'Excuse me, I was here ten minutes ago, and I think I left something you stick pins into, and it looks like this.' What came out was probably no more than 'please, large, photos, wall.'

Understandably the young girl was flummoxed, so she turned to her colleague at the next checkout counter who gladly interrupted her serving in order to draw some more clues out of me. When she had no success, despite my attempts to invent Spanish words for drawing pins, square, hang, useful, etc., she called the next cashier along the line. It was beginning to resemble a game of charades with me using hand gestures, depicting what to me was obviously a pinboard, but to them could have been anything from a car to a cupboard. I felt like a monkey in a zoo, with the public gawping and giggling at me through the bars. And the queues of customers were steadily growing.

After what seemed an age, a lady who had the bearing of the manager turned up. She was much better at charades, because almost at once she clicked her fingers and smiled, as if a light bulb had been turned on. She marched off to the back of the shop, the cashiers returned to their posts, and calm was restored. I waited and waited… to the point of thinking I could just slip out and forget the whole thing. Finally, though, she appeared from the back of the shop, all smiles, proudly clutching a huge cardboard box: 'La que usted busca, verdad?' (Just what you're looking for, correct?). 'Si, gracias!' I lied. I took the box and left.

Heading home, I was just pondering how to explain to Rose how I had managed to buy a pinboard, then lose a pinboard and acquire a huge box in its stead, when I passed the *farmácia*. I stopped in my tracks. 'Maybe...?' I went in and right there, leaning against the wall, was my pinboard.

'Es mío,' (it's mine) I told the pharmacist.

'Lo sé,' (I know) she said, with a sympathetic smile.

Part Two

Lacking the language and being as helpless as a baby in another culture has two advantages for the missionary... (1) it keeps you humble, and (2) it means you have to rely on other people. This in turn helps you make friends fast. Before long, two couples in our apartment block noticed how needy the new 'ingleses' (English people) were, and they were helping us in all manner of ways. They showed us where to buy postage stamps (pre-internet days, of course), how to enrol our young son into school (children start aged three in Spain) and how to call for a new *bombona* (gas bottle used for cooking and heating) when yours were running low. The latter required listening to the claxon of the *bombona* lorry and rushing out on to the balcony to attract the driver's attention by shouting down into the street. This does wonders for eroding natural British reserve.

One of the couples, Victor and Antonia (known as Toni), ran a local bar/restaurant, and they taught Rose how to cook

Spanish dishes in true local style – paella was Victor's speciality and Spanish tortilla was Toni's. We lived on the fourth floor and they on the third immediately below us, so the aroma of Spanish cooking was always wafting up from below. Our block had an enclosed internal courtyard, so as well as smells, there was a constant barrage of noise echoing round the internal walls. Early on, we were convinced all the neighbours were at war with one another because of the shouting, until we realised that high volume and explosive outbursts were part and parcel of everyday friendly Spanish conversation.

It was a small flat (sixty square metres) in the concrete jungle called Coslada – a Madrid suburb constructed in the Franco era to accommodate workers coming in from the countryside. The flat had ill-fitting windows and no central heating (hence the *bombonas*), which was a challenge in winter when temperatures dropped well below freezing. It was anything but peaceful, with a restless Alsatian dog above by day and a snoring man through the wall by night, but it was God's place for us and we thoroughly enjoyed the first two-and-a-half years of our time in Spain there. Victor and Toni, as well as Paco and Ester, were a great help to us in our vulnerability, teaching us a lot about Spanish culture, cuisine and language. I believe we gave them something in return – in spiritual, as well as friendship terms – but on one memorable occasion, we were able to be of practical support too ...

Late one evening I arrived back from a prayer meeting in another town, to find our whole street blocked off by a mass of people. I managed to find a parking space (not easy at the best of times) and walked the rest of the way. As I neared home, I noticed that everyone was looking in the same direction, upwards towards our apartment block. Then I caught sight of the fire engine and the smoke rising up into the night sky. With a sickening feeling, I realised the smoke was coming from the vicinity of our flat.

I pushed my way through the crowd toward the front door of the apartment block. As I arrived, a fireman in full firefighting gear, emerged through the door. 'No se puede entrar!' (You can't go in) he shouted through his facemask apparatus.

'Pero mi familia está dentro!' (But my family's inside) I replied.

'No se puede entrar!' he repeated and headed off towards the fire engine.

At last the crowd began to disperse, and the firemen started to withdraw and pack up their gear. I went in and sprinted up the four flights to our flat. The smoke hung heavy in the air and the smell was overpowering. 'What's happened?' I asked Rose as she opened the door. It transpired that the fire had broken out not in our flat, but in the flat below. Toni had left a frying pan with cooking oil on the stove, which had caught fire.

Rose takes up the story … 'That evening, I had just settled the children to bed and I decided to watch the Spanish news on TV. Sitting in the living room, I became aware of a lot of noise outside in the corridor. I went to the balcony and looked over to see a crowd of people looking up at me! I returned to the hallway of our flat and opened the door only to be met with noise and smoke. Shutting the door, I quickly decided to get the children up before shouting for help. This time when I re-opened the door, after this short period of time, we were now met with a wall of black, foul-smelling smoke. I shouted for help. A burly-looking fireman wearing a gas mask appeared around the corner and told me in no uncertain terms to 'Cierra la puerta, ya!' (Shut that door now!). The children and I backed off and did what he said. At least I knew that he knew we three were there. For what seemed like an age we waited, until Paul suddenly appeared.'

We put the children back to bed and Rose went downstairs to offer help. Toni was distraught, not just because of the devastation the fire had caused to her kitchen, but also at the thought of what might have happened to the neighbours. With no fire escape, no lift and only one stairwell, the danger to life was exacerbated. As Rose and Toni started clearing up, Victor arrived home from his evening shift in the bar. 'Pero … pero … qué ha pasado aquí?' (But … what's happened here?) he demanded, aghast and shaking his head in disbelief.

The sight was indeed shocking. The kitchen walls and ceiling were black, the appliances and cupboards were totally destroyed and there was a thick, grey layer of fire retardant everywhere, on the floor, windowsills, even the balcony outside the back door. Acrid smoke still hung in the air, inside the flat and in the enclosed courtyard outside.

Over the coming days, Rose was able to give practical help and emotional support to Toni. In time, they picked themselves up and had the kitchen refurbished. Dramatic and dangerous though it was, God brought good out of the situation, forging a strong relationship between us and our first Spanish neighbours. Yet again, it showed us that God brings blessings out of difficulties.

When we subsequently moved away to another town, it was not easy to say goodbye to these friends with whom we had shared support and encouragement in times of need. Many years have passed but we are so thankful that the Lord took us to that particular place at the beginning of our ministry in Spain.

'From one man **God** made every nation of people, that they should inhabit the whole earth; **and He determined the times set for them and the exact places where they should live.'** (Acts 17:26)

Paul and Rose Harvey were married in 1986 and, after working as a teacher and nurse respectively, and in local church work, they arrived in Spain in 1992.

AND FINALLY...

46

FROM RELUCTANT MISSIONARY

Edith Buxton

Edith Buxton (née Studd) was one of C. T. and Priscilla Studd's four daughters. She went out to the Belgian Congo (now the Democratic Republic of Congo) to marry Alfred Buxton, referring to herself as the 'reluctant missionary.' We finish this story collection with the account of her father and future husband in the forests of the Congo. Apart from it being an amusing episode in itself, it provides fascinating insight into the character of the founder of the Heart of Africa Mission, now known as WEC International.

Their journey now lay through the fierce Balenda tribe who had killed Emin Pasha. The surrounding tribes stood in unholy terror of them and it was difficult to get porters. The few who came only ventured to do so because they would be travelling with white men. A short while before, a white man had come across from Uganda. He was taken to the Chief Julu who stripped his clothes off, beat him and sent him back naked. Recently, too, an English elephant hunter had been shot by a native of his tribe with a poisoned arrow in the shoulder and he had died before he could get help.

'You'll never come through alive,' a trader warned them before they left.

C. T.'s reply was, 'They'll be too interested in our bicycles to do anything to us.'

'Bicycles!' cried the trader, 'so you mean to say you are going to bicycle through the jungle?'

'Certainly,' said C. T. 'We'll get to the other end more quickly. And when they can't carry us, we'll carry them.' He had an answer for everything and a faith big enough for any situation.

They must have looked an odd procession with C. T. and Alfred in knickerbockers in the middle of the African bush, riding their cycles when they could, and carrying them over the roots and stumps in their path when they couldn't. In this region one day, cycling on ahead, C. T. suddenly called to Alfred, 'Can you hear the porters?' There was dead silence. They had lost their way. They cycled back, there was no sign of them. Then the tracks crossed, and they took a wrong turn. On every side were massive trees, so tall they turned the midday sunshine to twilight. Vegetation steamed with heat.

A monkey or two swung from the lower branches gibbering at them. In the silence of the forest there were only the myriad sounds of tiny insects, birds and creaking branches. They felt as though a thousand eyes were staring through the thick bushes watching them. There was no doubt about it: they were lost in the primeval forest.

The dwellers of the forest, if they were to meet them, would be their enemies, hunters with poisoned arrows, perhaps even cannibals. For three hours they went this way and that; they had no idea where they were going, and the porters might now be twenty miles away.

Suddenly, they heard the snapping of twigs among the bushes. The next moment the trees parted and an almost naked African stood before them. In his hand he held a bow and some arrows.

His teeth were filed down to sharp points, the unmistakable mark of the cannibal. For what seemed hours, they stared at one another. Then C. T.'s gaze moved from the bow and arrow to the man's other hand. He carried a plaited basket and within it were some maize cobs and sweet potatoes.

C. T. stepped forward, the cannibal stepped back. C. T. pointed to the basket and then to their very empty stomachs. The man set down the basket and C. T. went forward again and picked up some of the potatoes. Neither he nor Alfred had any money on them. Suddenly an idea struck Father, as he looked down at his cycling breeches.

'Why have knickerbockers got so many buttons?' he demanded of the bewildered Alfred. 'I'll tell you; to give to undressed cannibals.'

In a moment he had ripped off half a dozen and given them to him. The man grinned and beckoned them to follow him. An hour or two later they were eating their dinner in the man's village. The food was well cooked by throwing it into the fire and pulling it out half an hour later, but they did not enquire what meat they were eating!

'A few more buttons settled the bill,' wrote Father. 'Their filed teeth declared our friends were indeed cannibals, but as both of us were lank, lean and tough, they were not tempted beyond what they were able; then we parted, Dei gratia, best of friends and amidst considerable applause.' Eventually, they were reunited with their porters and continued their journey.

From 'Reluctant Missionary' by Edith Buxton (1968, Lutterworth Press) pages 70–71.

RESOURCES

Books by WEC retired members

AN OPEN DOOR by Maud Kells (2019, 10Publishing, a division of 10ofthose.com)

GOD'S NEEDLE by Lily Gaynor & John Butterworth (2013, Monarch books)

ON GIANTS' SHOULDERS by Patrick McElligott (1991, 2002, Ambassador Publications)

Video interviews

Links to videos with Margaret Paton being interviewed by her son Timothée:

https://www.youtube.com/watch?v=uisaSqah9S8&t

https://www.youtube.com/watch?v=P67gc7bFWpY&t

Link to video of Richard Owens being interviewed by his grandson Andy in Japanese (with English subtitles):

https://www.youtube.com/watch?v=ejYBX7VL-RY&feature=youtu.be